Leadership, Conflict, and Cooperation in Afro-American Social Thought

Leadership, Conflict, and Cooperation in Afro-American Social Thought

JOHN BROWN CHILDS

Temple University Press

PHILADELPHIA

Temple University Press, Philadelphia 19122
Copyright © 1989 by Temple University. All rights reserved
Published 1989
Printed in the United States of America

The paper used in this publication meets the minimum
requirements of American National Standard for Information
Sciences—Permanence of Paper for Printed Library Materials,
ANSI Z39.48-1984

Library of Congress Cataloging-in-Publication Data

Childs, John Brown.
    Leadership, conflict, and cooperation in Afro-American social
thought / John Brown Childs.
        p.   cm.
    Bibliography: p.
    Includes index.
    ISBN 0-87722-581-8 (alk. paper) :
    1. Afro-American leadership.   2. Afro-Americans—Intellectual
life.   3. United States—Intellectual life—20th century.
4. Sociology—United States—History—20th century.   5. Social
action—United States—History—20th century.   I. Title.
E185.6.C534 1989
303.3'4'08996073—dc 19   88-12170   CIP

To Delgra Childs and to my mother, Dorothy Childs.

As for me, I have no blueprint for the future, but I know where I feel best.

Charles Denby
Indignant Heart,
A Black Worker's Journal

Contents

Preface   xi

1. Two World Views   3

2. Constituting the Vanguard: Washington and
   Du Bois Imagine Leading Groups, Each in
   His Own Image   10

3. *The Messenger* and *The New Negro*   48

4. Non-Elite Social Action: George W. Ellis,
   Arturo Schomburg, and the Universal Negro
   Improvement Association   81

5. From the 1960s into the Future   123

   Notes   149

   Index   163

Preface

Why is it that those who oppose oppression often save their most bitter, and sometimes violent, attacks for one another? Why does the fight for justice often adopt elitist rather than egalitarian approaches, authoritarian rather than cooperative methods, dogmatic rather than flexible outlooks? What can be done among diverse groups to encourage egalitarian forms of social action that are in keeping with the goal of ending subjugation and creating a just society?

In this work, I analyze these issues as they emerge in black American social thought from the turn of the century through the 1920s. I also suggest how we may approach egalitarian cooperation and examine the implications for contemporary social change.

I approach this topic as an anthropologist, not as a political scientist or a historian. My interest here is not with "politics" but with what anthropologists call "world view." As Clifford Geertz puts it, such analysis of world views involves investigation of peoples' "most comprehensive ideas of order" and their "concepts of nature, of self, of society."[1] Consequently, I want to get beyond the smoke and fire of highly visible political battles to discern the deeper, less visible, conceptual currents beneath. I do not seek to reconstruct past social reality or paint a picture of what life was like "back then." I do not attempt to survey all social-philosophical positions of all black writers, but to select examples that will help reveal new patterns.

Central to this work is my deep concern that movement toward a just and egalitarian society not be subverted by authoritarian tendencies, that the drive for openness not be lost in rigid closed perspectives, and that the call for unity not be a cloak behind which one group seeks to direct the rest. I believe it is possible and necessary to have many different modes of action, tactics, and strategies that reflect diverse participants in social movements. I hope that this book will point to the need for such diversity within egalitarian social movements and also help to achieve it.

Although writing a book is a solitary venture, I have benefited from a wide range of commentary on my work. Naturally, all mistakes and misinterpretations are my own. I am deeply grateful to Jill Cutler, Jeremy Brecher, and Martin Bresnick for their incisive analysis of the various stages of this writing. Hardy T. Frye and Henry Louis Gates were early and valued supporters of this project. I want to thank Ernest J. Allen, Harold Cruse, James O'Connor, Roberto Marquez, Andrew Parker, and William J. Wilson for their suggestions. Two anonymous readers for Temple University Press also provided thoughtful remarks. The research people at the New York Public Library's Schomburg Center for Research in Black Culture were informed and generous in their assistance. An Andrew W. Mellon Faculty Fellowship at Harvard University provided me with invaluable sabbatical time to conduct a major portion of my research. Michael Ames of Temple University Press was a supportive and sharply perceptive editor. Charles de Kay, production editor at Temple University Press, provided finely crafted work on the final phases of this endeavor. Finally, Kluwer Academic Publishers granted permission to reprint sections of my work that appeared in *Theory and Society* 13 (1984).

Leadership, Conflict,
and Cooperation
in Afro-American
Social Thought

1

Two World Views

Vanguard groups are the modern messiahs. They claim access to special knowledge revealed only to the initiated. About them wafts the aroma of purity that distinguishes them from the very masses they intend to lead. And they have a great mission of fundamental change.

The Vanguard Perspective assumes the basic energy, the essential vitality of the people. In this view the people are raw, basic, and of the earth. But like natural resources, the energy of the people is subject to exploitation by the dominant society. Their energy can be used by others to maintain the status quo.

The people are seen as totally vulnerable. They have no sense of their past, no understanding of the present, and no vision of the future. In a word, they lack consciousness. The Vanguard's essential task is to lift the people out of the stage of unconscious dormant energy and to give them an awareness of their own strength by directing them in how to act. The sleeping masses cannot undertake such a task themselves. Instead, their awakening must be accomplished by a group that is outside the state of sleep immobilizing them. This group is imbued with a special knowledge of how the liberation of the people is to take place.

This special group, the Vanguard, holds that there is within society a dominant center from which all else flows. To make positive basic changes in society, it is necessary to understand and control this center. Those within the Vanguard, however, differ in how they identify the dominant

3

center. Those who identify the center as materialistic seek to control economic power and the structures of science and technology. Those who see the center as idealistic seek to control society's culture—its philosophy, art, and literature.

Those who take the materialistic view believe that culture is dangerously divorced from reality. Those who take the idealistic view agree that the cultural realm is to some degree separate from the everyday world, but hold that it is just this distinctness that gives culture its liberating edge. The consciousness must be freed before any economic, scientific, or technological change can take place. Even in the midst of oppression, the Vanguard can, through culture, develop the means of control before actual social modifications have been made. The materialistic view, in contrast, holds that any transformation in consciousness, manifested in art and literature, will follow "real" changes in the economic and scientific realms.

Both of these important divergent views in the Vanguard thus accept the idea of a dominant center in society and assume that control over this center will lead to changes in the remainder of society. Through their understanding and control of the central arena, the group that has grasped the true significance of the center will direct the masses of people toward their liberation.

The Vanguard thus both respects and disdains the masses. It respects the energy of the masses as a vital propellant for change, yet it disdains the apparent vulnerability of the masses, which seem to lack creative consciousness. The masses are a dull blade that the Vanguard must sharpen and wield as the sword of liberation. The possibility that contributions to the struggle might come from a diverse spectrum within the oppressed population, contributions that would stand equal with the Vanguard's own, is not considered.

Indeed, the Vanguard seeks to inhibit the direct influence of the masses on decision making. The Vanguard lays down a guideline, a blueprint, that the others must follow. Those of the masses who possess more initiative will adapt themselves to the plan with some brilliance but they will do so as followers. So restrictive is this blueprint that being in the educated strata of society is by no means sufficient to gain membership in the Vanguard group. Whatever one's social origins, there must be strict adherence to the plan.

The Vanguard aims at the creation of a closed social movement within which the guidelines of the leading group are faithfully followed. The rules of interaction should be accepted by all engaged in the struggle. Initiative, courage, and determination are welcomed by the leading group as long as they do not depart from the basic standard discourse. There is not much room for "play"—the fluid improvisations of many different actors who try now one and now another approach.

An immediate result of this requirement that those who want to build must follow the blueprint is a clear sense of boundary between those who follow the plan and those who do not. This sense of boundary is what gives the Vanguard its aroma of purity. The guidelines exclude randomness, unpredictability, and all other options. The plan provides a complete mode of action and thought. The entrant is purified, escaping from framelessness and inaccurate frameworks, entering the one channel that offers the means to struggle effectively and with certainty.

Because there is only one blueprint for action, and only one group that has access to that blueprint, no other approach can be tolerated. Each group assumes that there is one Vanguard perspective—the "correct" one. All others are viewed as false messiahs bearing fraudulent messages. Thus the Vanguard perspective is fundamentally exclusionary and sets up internecine struggles among groups that actually have a great deal in common.

It is not the differences between various Vanguard approaches that are the problem. The real problem is the characteristic effort of each particular Vanguard group to shape all others into its own image and to reject those who take different approaches. Those who take different approaches quite naturally fight back, and so potential allies join battle in heated disarray.

The excusionary Vanguard concept of political action recalls the medieval European view of the universe as centered on the earth—the earth in this case being the plan of a particular group. The alternative is the Mutuality concept, which resembles the Renaissance view of Giordano Bruno —who saw the universe as a complex of many worlds that has no one center.[1]

Imagine, if you will, many groups of people hacking their way through a dense forest from different directions, all seeking escape from oppression. They have no knowledge of one another. Each group believes itself to be isolated. At last they begin to hear the voices of others, indistinct at first, then clearer, as the groups chop their way through the thickets. Even before they can actually see one another they call out greetings and stories of their struggle. Directions are exchanged. Progress is reported. Arguments erupt. Some groups are riddled with dissension; others are harmonious. Nonetheless, they have a growing understanding of being in motion with many others. They draw closer.

Suddenly all their chopping and hacking produces an extraordinary result. As they move, the thick brush falling before them, they create, at the very moment of meeting, a gigantic clearing. For the first time they all see each other; they move to embrace; they can talk face to face. In contrast to the obscurity of the forest through which they have passed, the clearing is open to the light.

The separate movements could have wandered sporadically, never meeting, for the impelling force of oppression is not itself a guide toward greater closeness with others. It was their voices, at first indistinct over great distance, and then increasingly clear and meaningful, that allowed a common direction to develop. This direction did not lead them to an already established place, a fabled El Dorado. There was no clearing in the forest awaiting them. Rather, as they drew closer they created the place and the moment of clearing. For that revolutionary moment there can be no precise map, no timetable, no all-knowing guide. All must contribute to its coming-into-being; none can, in isolation, make it happen.

But even as they congratulate themselves on their creation through struggle, more voices are heard. Others are clearing the forest nearby. Those in the different clearings call to one another. They again pick up their machetes and cut through the thickness. Another larger clearing suddenly emerges. There is celebration. Then, from off in the distance, still more voices—

The correspondence of all groups and domains has two related meanings. First, "correspondence" refers to the actual social-historical currents within which diverse groups of people live. The very diversity of those who experience inequality and subjugation indicates how widespread that pattern is. It was this sense of shared experience, cutting across class lines, that led Malcolm X to remind the people in his audiences, "Whether you are educated or illiterate, whether you live on the boulevard or the alley, you are going to catch hell just like I am."[2] Many people around the world share the experience of injustice. The holding of such feelings is a basic reality that brings widely separated peoples into correspondence at a social-historical level.

But such social-historical correspondence does not guarantee a recognition of commonality among peoples. To the contrary, people are more prone to accentuate differences and lose track of parallels. Common feelings of subjugation, of being treated unfairly by those with power, do not necessarily result in recognition of others as companion sufferers. The sense of social-historical commonalities must be *communicated* among diverse groups. In a second sense, groups must *correspond* with one another. Information about the particular forms of inequality, subjugation, and resistance must be shared.

Such correspondence leads toward a horizontal expansion of groups in ever-widening cooperative union. This brings us to an important feature of Mutuality. There is no room for a leading group in this approach. Everyone has the capacity for conscious analysis and the envisioning of a better world.

If, in this view, there is no one directing group with "the special knowledge," it is because there is in reality no one dominant center. The economy is no less and no more important than the construction of ideas in literature; the political realm is no more significant than the philosophical or the artistic.

The objective, therefore, is not to develop a leading group. Rather, it is to expand the mutual recognition and interaction of a multitude of groups, all of whom have undergone oppression. This formulation differs fundamentally from Vanguard assumptions. Here there are no impermeable boundaries between groups. No one group is "pure," for there is no special knowledge that would put one group in superior position to set the rules for everyone else.

The mutual interaction approach is anti-parochial and yet pro-local. While some intellectuals may, for example, have a broad understanding of the world, they may be ignorant of what it is like to struggle as a longshoreman, a cook, or a sharecropper. Intellectuals, like others, are local in their knowledge.

Each separate group constantly reaches out to the wider world of other groups, and it welcomes the particular contribution that each group can make from its own vantage point. In becoming aware of and acting with others, each group enhances itself by ending its isolation and embedding itself in a larger, more powerful process.

The many different viewpoints included in Mutuality must admit key elements from the Vanguard perspective as well. The Vanguard alertness to the effects of long-term subjugation on people, its understanding of the issues of capitalism, class, and race, will prevent Mutuality from becoming a mushy liberalism in which all work together without any alteration in the status quo. If Mutuality warns us against looking to a leading all-knowing group for salvation, the Vanguard perspective warns us against accepting every action uncritically. As Antonio Gramsci observes, freedom must be protected provided it is not "the 'freedom' to exploit."[3] Thus a Mutualistic viewpoint does not reject the Vanguard Perspective as an enemy. Rather it is seen as a vital tendency, containing elements that can be incorporated into more egalitarian modes of action.

Diversity, the particularity of different groups, the distinctiveness and usefulness of their contributions can be seen, not as barriers but as essential elements in social change. Different agendas are not the basic problem. It is the effort to put one agenda's priorities into effect over those of other agendas that causes conflict. It is not the unity of one vantage point, one detailed plan, that is needed. Instead, we need room for a range of very different participants who create social change through their mutual interaction. The demand for unity, which sounds positive, must always be received with caution. Who is making the demand, and from whose position is the particular brand of unity being pushed? Mutuality reaches out to tap the positive element in that demand—which is nothing other than the effort to expand the strength of the isolated by combining forces. But Mutuality, as a fluid and flexible form of action and thought, must allow for continued diversity and disunity. Mutuality celebrates contradiction.

All mutual action will of necessity be extremely difficult, tension-filled, and shifting because it is free. Concomitantly, mutual action can only have real effect if it is also coherent and shared, in a word—cooperative.

Because Mutuality involves a constant egalitarian mode of action, it is not simply a march toward a better future. Rather each step—however minute, however personal—brings the future to life in the present. Certainly we cannot be satisfied to simply replicate the hierarchical power madness of the society we seek to transform. Equality is not a goal to be reached. It is both goal and method; it is the means of reaching and also that toward which we strive.

Mississippi civil rights activist Fannie Lou Hamer tells of her meeting with the young workers of the Student Non-Violent Coordinating Committee (SNCC). Instead of finding them to be "leaders" who would try to direct her, she found people who recognized her as a disciplined, creative, and resilient person and who took her own experiences of oppression and resistance very seriously. "They told me," she says, " 'Now look, Mrs. Hamer, you're the people living in Mississippi, we don't have to tell you nothing, you make your own decisions.' " For Hamer that moment was part of the progress toward true freedom. "See, we'd never been allowed to do that before. Cause you see, if we are free people as Negroes, if we are free, then I don't think you're supposed to tell me how much of my freedom I'm supposed to have."[4]

To act and learn through mutual respect rather than to give orders is crucial to the struggle. Such cooperative egalitarian action, such Mutuality, is itself a victory.

2

Constituting
the Vanguard

Washington and Du Bois
Imagine Leading Groups,
Each in His Own Image

Booker T. Washington and W. E. B. Du Bois, whom most
commentators consider exact opposites, engaged in sometimes bitter debate, especially concerning education. Du
Bois, seen by many as a progressive radical critic, looked on
Washington as an apologist for the status quo. Washington's
approach seemed to him vocational training for servants.

The *Messenger* magazine, socialist voice of A. Philip Randolph and Chandler Owen, concurred that Washington was
indeed one of the "Old Crowd" who opposed radical change
—but they included Du Bois in that same category, especially after Du Bois called for black people to close ranks
with white America in the First World War fight against
Germany. These differences were forgotten, however, when
the "Old Crowd" Du Bois and the "radical" *Messenger*
joined forces to oust Marcus Garvey from his position of
influence among black people. They shared an animosity
toward Garvey so intense that they co-authored a letter to
the Justice Department detailing allegations against him,
hoping that the government would deport him, which it
eventually did in 1927. Garvey in turn cast aspersions on
what he termed "the mulatto elite" of Du Bois and others.

Meanwhile, more quietly but no less significantly, Alain Locke and Charles Johnson, among others, were organizing the manifesto of the black literati, artists, and other intellectuals—the *New Negro*. This work purported to depict the true leading elite elements of the "race" while ignoring much of what the *Messenger* and Garvey were doing.

What are we to make of these twistings and turnings?

One common approach is to locate the combatants along a political spectrum that runs from "conservative" to "radical" as well as from "separatist" to "integrationist." For example, Washington can be seen as a conservative who was opposed by the radical Du Bois. Unfortunately, this categorization does not help us to comprehend the *Messenger*'s lumping them together as "Old Crowd Negroes." We might try to slip out of this dilemma by pushing the *Messenger* further to the left on the spectrum, saying that they were more radical than Du Bois. But we still are at a loss when we confront the *Messenger*-Du Bois alliance against Garvey.

Our problem here is that terms such as "radical" and "conservative" do not really apply. If, however, we try the concepts of the Vanguard perspective and Mutuality, we may uncover some interesting patterns.

What was the situation like in turn-of-the-century America for black activists who sought to improve the condition of black people? Racist policies had been enshrined in law and driven into the flesh of black America through torture and massacre. The larger part of the black population, many born in slavery, had been brutally deprived of basic civil liberties. In the most minute ways, the lives of millions of black people were subject to totalitarian controls, down to the very expressions on their faces. Not casting one's eyes down, a sidewise glance from black man to white woman, a proffered handshake from black to white could result in beatings or murder. Within this Orwellian environment of painstakingly detailed subjugation, much of it hidden behind the Cotton Curtain of the South, leaders such as Booker T. Washington, and W. E. B. Du Bois struggled to develop strategies that could cope with existing conditions while working to overturn them. Slavery had, from Washington's and Du Bois's viewpoints, eroded the capacity of black people in general to organize themselves. Consequently, it would not be possible to challenge the status quo without firm guidance from small elite portions of the black population who through education and "breeding" were not subject to the cancer of oppression.

Writing about the internal difficulties faced by the black masses after slavery, Du Bois argued that the "Negro, however, had two especial difficulties: his training as a slave and freedman has not been such as to make the average of the race as efficient and reliable workmen as the average native [white] American or as many foreign immigrants."[1] Then, noting that these problems were rooted in the impact of slavery on black consciousness, Du Bois added, "This is without doubt to be expected in a people who for generations have been trained to shirk work."[2] A peculiar notion actually—that slaves, whose daily existence was one of labor-on-demand had been "trained" to shirk work. In this passage Du Bois does not allude to examples of creative sabotage of the work process by recalcitrant slaves.

Turn-of-the-century black leaders faced a situation not unlike that which confronted the Bolsheviks in the twilight of Czarist Russia. A large mass of apparently backward people, whose capacity for disciplined analysis and self-government seemed deeply retarded by long years of oppression, were to be guided toward change. Elite progressives would have to be the catalysts for positive change.

It is in this general context that answers to the question of who was to create the knowledge and organization necessary for progress were fashioned in various ways by Washington and Du Bois, and somewhat later by the architects of the *Messenger* and the *New Negro*.

But in fact, these downtrodden masses had a real capacity for organization. Through the work of historians such as John Hope Franklin, John Blassingame, and Albert Raboteau, today we know just how organized black communities had been during slavery. We also know, through the work of writers such as Peter Rachleff, about the post–Civil War growth of important grass-roots black organizations that drew from local communities without the aid of black elites. Certainly, indigenous organizations, such as those created by black guerrillas among the Seminoles up through the post–Civil War Colored Farmers Alliance, testify to the capacity of ordinary people to create structures for resistance and survival.[3]

How does the Vanguard view such organization? It views it as "spontaneity"—the blind fury of the oppressed, passion without thought, action without the necessary structure. "Spontaneity," said derisively, is another way of implying that the oppressed have a vital energy but need guidance —hence the role for the Vanguard. But the problem with such a notion of spontaneity is that it ignores the real organizational basis on which popular action actually takes place. What looks like spontaneous eruption to a shocked group of would-be leaders is often well thought out action.

Indeed, it is the reality of indigenous organization that accounts for the usually vehement Vanguard reaction against popular action. The problem is not that such activity is spontaneous and unorganized. The problem is that the Vanguard finds itself competing with existing organizations created by the people themselves. This was precisely the dilemma confronting the Bolshevik vanguard in its confrontation with the peasant movement led by Lester Makno.[4]

On the other hand, organizations that develop among the oppressed may include certain predatory forms such as gangsterism, drug pushing, and pimping. This too is part of the reality of the harsh world in which many of the subjugated must survive. Such realities give Vanguard claims a certain plausibility. Furthermore, if there was any moment in Afro-American history when a Vanguard tendency could find justification in the real ground of existing circumstances, then turn-of-the-century America was it. Reeling from the aftermath of slavery and the bloody dismantling of Reconstruction gains, locked into semi-feudal cycles of servitude as sharecroppers, cut off from other black people by the Cotton Curtain, denied access to meaningful education and employment, beginning to move to the cities with all the attendant dislocations of that urbanization— black people indeed found their position difficult. Vanguard assertions of the importance of educated elite leadership were not unfounded. Nonetheless, the elites exaggerated the need for their services by ignoring equally real examples of popular community organization. This fabricated dimension in their claims for leadership must always be kept in sight.

It is within this context of semi-real, semi-fabricated claims of mass disorganization and impotence that the question as to who was to create the knowledge necessary for progressive action was answered in diverse but characteristically Vanguard fashion by Washington, Du Bois, the *Messenger* editors, and the *New Negro* authors.

Booker T. Washington's Industrialists, Financiers, and Technocrats

Washington and Du Bois agreed on the need for a Vanguard group. They had quite different ideas regarding the membership of such a group. Let us first examine Washington's requirements for leadership of the black masses.

There was a tough side to Booker T. Washington. For him, it was not sufficient that black people gain the respect of white people by succeeding in business. Black people would have to seize economic power in the South. In Washington's view, banks would depend on black investments and the white population would come to need the industrial and agricultural services of powerful black financiers and farmers. As a producer, the black man was to "make the white man dependent" upon him.[5] Consequently, it was of vital importance to Washington that there be black people who could take control of the Southern economy. He did not expect black farmers and craftspeople to carry out the vast changes that he felt were coming; in fact,

> Just now the need is not so much for common carpenters, brick-masons, farmers, and laundry-women as for industrial leaders, men who in addition to their practical knowledge, can draw plans, make estimates, take contracts. . . .[6]

The economic control that such leaders could accumulate would allow black people to constrain racism:

We complain a great deal, and rightly, about the treatment accorded us on the railroads of public carriers in some parts of our country. We should remember, however, that the securities that largely govern these public carriers are on the market, and are as easily bought by black men as by white, and that the men who own the securities in the long run control the policy of the public carriers.[7]

Washington uses the words "govern" and "control." This is no humble request for "separate but equal treatment." Rather it is a tough strategy for wielding economic power. If blacks could gain such control it would matter little whether whites liked them. Washington wrote, "When a black man is the largest taxpayer and owns and cultivates the most successful farm in his county, his white neighbors will not object very long to his voting and to having his vote honestly counted."[8]

The economic system, Washington said, lay at the foundation of all other aspects of society; hence, black economic power would ultimately lead to black political strength. All of this would take place within the embrace of capitalism: technology and methods developed by Northern scientists and technicians would improve agriculture; capitalist money would fuel the development of industry; the drive for profit, coupled with the activity of capitalists, would sweep aside racist sentiment.

Thus there was more to Washington's thought than merely an admonition that black people wait for the whites to come to their senses. Nor was Washington merely an apologist for the status quo. He argued for a hard-headed acceptance of facts "as they were" while also believing that those facts would change, or more exactly, be blown to pieces by powerful forces of economic development. There was no need, argued Washington, to engage in futile political gestures. The political system was itself a prisoner of the irrationality of racism and so could not possibly be the forum for practical activity of any consequence. Black people could not gain power by "artificial forcing" such as politicking.

In taking this position, Washington did not suggest that other aspects of life were not important.

> I know that what I have said will likely suggest the idea that I have put stress upon the lower things of life— the material; that I have overlooked the higher side, the ethical and religious. I do not overlook or undervalue the higher. All that I advocate in this article is not as an end but as a means. I know as a race we have got to be patient in the laying of a firm foundation, that our tendency is too often to get the shadow instead of the substance, the appearance rather than the reality.[9]

It is characteristic of Washington's thought to emphasize laying a "firm foundation," meaning an economic one, as the basis for all other political, social, and cultural development. His imagery throughout is materialistic and concrete. He emphasizes "substance" instead of "shadow," "reality" rather than "appearance." "Without a solid economic foundation," he wrote, "it is impossible for any race of people to make much enduring, much permanent progress."[10] This economic foundation lay at the bottom of "religion, education, and politics."[11] Washington's image of the solid economic foundation upon which society must be built parallels Marxist notions of economic base and ideological superstructure. Because of his focus on a solid base, which required both time and patience to construct, many have called Washington a "gradualist." But from Washington's point of view, the laying of an economic foundation was essential however long it took.

Washington's was not a simple, deterministic view in which people are carried along by huge historic currents. He thought that people could play conscious, active roles in shaping history. Yet it was also possible, in his view, for history to pass a people by. If a people were not scientifically aware of the significance of the developing economic circumstances, they would not be able to benefit from those changes. People could take advantage of the historic moment if they were alert to the developments unfolding beneath them. Such awareness would not come easy for it would require taking a long view, looking beyond the immediate present. This was why Washington insisted on "industrial training." He did not seek to turn black people into more effective servants. Quite the contrary, there was a historic need, he argued, for leaders who could prepare the black masses to take a controlling role in history. Such leaders would concentrate on economic development since it was at that fundamental level that the transformation of the South would take place.

Washington foresaw, as did certain circles of "enlightened" Southerners, a "New South" filled with economic vitality pumped in by the growing industrial might of Northern capitalism. But he was looking further than the opportunities offered by industrialization. He had an image of the revolutionary power of capitalism to overturn precapitalist backwardness. The global tendency, he believed, was against such backwardness and toward economic development and progress. When Washington imagined black people playing an active role in remaking the South, he was also imagining them as actors in the global drama of capitalism. How could racism, in the Southern backwater, stand up against a force so mighty that it had swept the aristocracies of England and France into the dustbin of history? Alert black leaders, conscious of the power of capitalist development, would have to be poised to act.

W. E. B. Du Bois's Enlightened Warriors

In Du Bois's classic book of essays, *The Souls of Black Folk*, there is a telling passage whose significance is often overlooked. In the chapter, "Of the Faith of the Fathers," Du Bois describes his visit to an Afro-American religious revival meeting. It is a true down-home gathering. We can almost hear the cicadas in the background as Du Bois approaches. Folks are ready to express themselves, to jump and shout, to feel the Lord, and to enjoy the sharing of belief. Du Bois, however, stands apart, like one of the outsider figures in a Breughel painting, observing but not participating. He is close at hand, yet we feel the great distance between him and the people. For Du Bois it is a moment of emotional eruption, a departure from rational thought. Du Bois writes, "A sort of suppressed terror hung in the air and seemed to seize us—a divine madness, a demonic possession, that lent a terrible reality to song and word."[12]

Despite his use of the term "us," nowhere does Du Bois describe himself as partaking of the "pythian madness" of the country folk around him. Rather he observes their apparent frenzy, as if from afar: "The people moaned and fluttered, and then the gaunt-cheeked brown woman beside me suddenly leaped straight into the air and shrieked like a lost soul, while round about came wail and groan and outcry and a scene of human passion such as I had never conceived before."[13]

Such images of popular passion are important in Du Bois's outlook. For him the people were a source of vital energy, but that energy lacked the necessary direction for progress. For Du Bois, as for Washington, the problem was how to tie popular energy to elite leadership. Du Bois's plan called for an elite different from that of Washington's. His leading group would not be technocrats and industrialists but cultured warriors. They would be cosmopolitan, free from the constrictions of any particular society. For them, world literature, art, and philosophy—in a word, "culture"—would form a free zone, untrammeled by the tendency toward crass materialism that Du Bois felt characterized Washington's approach.

This free zone of culture was not for everyone. It was only the "advance guard" of the race that "toiled slowly, heavily, doggedly" up "the new path."[14] This cadre of black people, "emancipated by training and culture,"[15] was unique and distinct from the broader black population and from the overall black elite. Theirs was a true emancipation, won through the liberation of the self. Once achieved it could not be taken away.

This advance guard, however, could not isolate itself within its own uniqueness. The "thinking classes," said Du Bois, had a "responsibility to the struggling masses."[16] This was no pious exhortation to show concern for the benighted underclass. Du Bois's call to the vanguard involved not a plea but an imperative. The black vanguard had no choice but to lift the struggling masses from oppression. By the very act of taking part in the culture of resistance, the vanguard became not an elite disdainful of the "mob" but revolutionary leaders at the head of a long march. Within the stronghold glowed the profound reality of the total transformation of the self, the creation of the new person who would feel duty bound to serve the people:

> We are training not isolated men, but a living group of men,—nay a group within a group. And the final product of our training must neither be a psychologist or a brickmason, but a man. And to make men, we must have ideals, broad, pure and inspiring ends of living.[17]

"Neither be psychologist nor a brickmason"—the cadre was to consist of whole individuals capable of embracing both the analytic and the emotional, the pragmatic and the rarefied. And, at the heart of this elite was idealism. For Du Bois, such a black vanguard would be superior to Washington's technicians and businessmen.

We must not confuse this radical stronghold of culture and its enlightened warriors with the "talented tenth." Certainly, Du Bois adopted that term as did many others. In its broadest sense, it could include both Washington's financiers and technocrats and Du Bois's cultural warriors. But from Du Bois's perspective, only a section of the black elite, one that had torn itself free from the merely "talented" ones in order to become resisters to capitalism and agents for change, could be the vanguard. This vanguard would be known not only by its worldly success but by its transformation of the soul and the mind, and by its forging of philosophical weapons with which black people would be led to liberation.

Washington constructed a vanguard in his own image. He was knowledgeable about technology, conversant with industrialists, and understanding of the spirit of capitalism.

In contrast, Du Bois's vanguard, like him, would be highly literate, cosmopolitan, and well-versed in the world's high culture. Both men envisioned their vanguard groups in ways that would privilege a particular portion of the black elite and exclude others. Both men essentially excluded the black masses. The issue for them was which portion of the black elite was to occupy the main leadership positions. The possibility of local grass-roots leadership, arising from many sources, was not considered.

Booker T. Washington and the Seizure of Economic Power

Washington's premise was that racism was irrational and abnormal. White businessmen were actually losing money in order to uphold racist beliefs: "On most other subjects white men use their reason, not their feelings; but in considering the subject of the colored man, in most cases, there are evidences of passion—a tendency to exaggerate and to make a sensation of the most innocent and meaningless events."[18] Washington suggested that their profits would increase if they would only come to their senses: "This unjust practice toward the negro cuts off thousands of dollars worth of negro travel every year, while just treatment of the negro would stop no white travel."[19] Nor was it merely the railroads, important as they were, that were working against the businessmen's best interests. The entire South was suffering economically and would continue to suffer because of racist beliefs. The most fundamental evidence of this irrationality was the loss of the Southern black work force to the Northern cities.

Yet Washington's was hardly a simple plea to whites to come to their senses. Unlike their Southern counterparts, Northern businessmen seemed cold, calculating, and driven by the desire for profit. Washington did not condemn them; he approved of them. He argued that the incisive clarity of profit-driven capitalism was precisely the means by which the sensational emotional appeals of racism could be destroyed. Washington's views paralleled the contention of Marx and Engels in the *Communist Manifesto* that capitalism has "pitilessly torn asunder the motley feudal ties that bound man to his 'natural superiors' and has left remaining no other nexus between man and man than naked self-interest, than callous 'cash payment.'"[20] Similarly for Washington, "it is surprising to see how quickly sentiment and prejudice will disappear under the influence of hard cash."[21] Against hard cash, "sentiment" could not defend itself, for "the dollar has not an ounce of sentiment in it."[22]

Washington did not see the primary task as convincing racists to be tolerant. Rather the task was to revolutionize the South physically and economically with modern capitalist organization, uprooting archaic backward Southern society with the power of the machine. There would be tremendous changes in agriculture; old-fashioned inequitable sharecropping and inefficient agricultural techniques would be replaced by modern science and management that would improve the living conditions of black people. Simultaneously, there would be an increasing industrialization of the Southern cities and an acceleration in the production of primary resources such as coal and iron.

Washington was fascinated by the potential of scientific modes of production. In his view, scientifically mechanized agriculture would accomplish two major objectives: the work would be made more efficient and humane; and white farmers would be drawn into economic relations on a parity with black farmers. Washington foreshadowed the efforts by modern third-world nations to escape the limitations of single-crop agriculture when he argued for the diversification of crops:

> For years all acknowledge that the South has suffered from the low prices of cotton because of overproduction. The economic history of the world teaches that an ignorant farming class means a single crop, and that a single crop means, too often, low prices from overproduction or famine from underproduction.[23]

This diversification would protect black people from both the perils of over- and underproduction. Rather than simply being an advocate of sturdy yeoman farmers, as many see him, Washington was a proponent of the idea that agriculture had to be considered an industry that required a high degree of sophisticated technological and scientific knowledge. "We have got to put brain into agricultural pursuits," he declared, "not merely the sweat of our brawn without any profit."[24]

Agricultural machinery, which allowed one man to ac-

complish the work of many men, would transform the agriculture of the South by changing its cultivation pattern from
plots to fields, from vulnerable cotton to diversified crops.
The students at Tuskegee, said Washington, were being
taught to "master the forces of nature" through science:

> In a word the constant aim is to show the student how
> to put brains into every process of labour, how to bring
> his knowledge of mathematics and the sciences in farm-
> ing, carpentry, forging, foundry-work, how to dispense as
> soon as possible with the old form of *ante-bellum* labour.[25]

The industrializing of agriculture would be paralleled by improvements in production and refinement of raw materials.
Mines would be opened and great factories built. Already,
suggested Washington, citing statistics furnished by one of
the coal companies in Alabama, large numbers of black people were working as miners. Ninety percent of Southern
coal was produced by black workers.[26]

The advance of capitalism in the South would bring many
benefits to black people. The absence of unions in the South
both made it congenial terrain for the industrialists and removed one of the artificial barriers to black employment
that existed in the North. The task before black people was
to prepare themselves for the outburst of capitalist development in the South. "Cast your buckets down where you
are," Washington urged, adding:

> The colored man's present great opportunity in the South
> is in the matter of business, and success here is going
> to constitute the foundation for success and relief along
> other lines. . . . Any colored man with common sense,
> a reasonable education and business ability, can take
> $1,000 in cash and go into any Southern community, and
> in five years be worth $5,000. He does not meet with
> that stern, relentless competition that he does when he
> butts up against the Northern Yankee. The black man
> can sooner conquer Southern prejudice than Northern
> competition.[27]

The problem was how to overcome the barriers that
would stop black people from taking up their historic role
and gaining their freedom. Washington believed that the

barriers were to be found in what today would be called false consciousness. He staunchly attacked what he viewed as an illusory and corrosive faith in politics and culture among key sectors of the black leadership. His critique of culture stands in especial contrast to Du Bois's emphasis on art, literature, and philosophy.

Washington argued that black involvement with Western literature, poetry, and painting was at best a luxury and at worst a damaging illusion of potency. What appeared to be progress—in the form of a black intellectual elite schooled in the arts—was for Washington a retrograde, even reactionary development that was sapping the strength of black intellectuals and depriving the race of necessary leadership.

An essential element in Washington's critique of culture was his distinction between "shadow and substance." The base of everything was practical action in the material world. Above that foundation, all else was secondary at best and illusory at worst. The most visible example of such superficiality was to be found, suggested Washington, in the foppish mannerisms of the city slickster:

> Out in the state of Kansas there are two former acquaintances of mine, both of whom left Alabama about twenty or twenty-five years ago; one of them settled in the country and went to farming; the other found employment in the city. Not long since, I journeyed through the state of Kansas, and I met the one who had remained in the city. He was pretty well dressed, had on a nice suit of clothes, pants all creased and of the proper cut, beautiful necktie, cuffs, right up-to-date, stylish hat and shoes, and, in short, he looked as if he might be very propsperous; but when I began to ask him some questions I found that outside of his new fashioned clothes he had not accumulated anything since he had left the South.[28]

In contrast, the country man, a man who began "at the bottom" by working the land had "after a few years of hardship" come to own a beautiful farm and was the head of a substantial and happy family. Without this grounding in the soil, without a start at the bottom, all that would be acquired would be the shadow, not the substance—culture being equated with the shadow.

Washington complained of the superficiality of culture in an 1896 address at the Armstrong-Slater Memorial Trade School:

> One value of industrial education is in the fact that without it we are likely to get hold of a superficial culture. In proportion to our means we have more culture than any other people. But culture out of all proportion to our means, culture without a decent home and a bank account means little.[29]

In this fashion, Washington mounted his assault on those whom he considered to be cultured "out of all proportion" to reality. An excessive emphasis on learning dead languages such as ancient Greek and Latin or on poetry and plays of the classic European writers served no practical purpose, he argued. Those who engaged in such cultured activity were fooling themselves.

Washington never tired of aphoristic stories of the cultured young man or woman living in the midst of terrible poverty but made oblivious to its harsh realities by the siren song of *belles lettres:*

> I was amazed to find that it was almost impossible to find an educated colored man who could teach the making of clothing. We could find numbers of them who could teach astronomy, theology, Latin or grammar, but almost none who could instruct in the making of clothing, something that has to be used by every one of us every day of the year. How often have I been discouraged as I have gone through the South, and into the homes of the people of my race, and have found women who could converse intelligently upon abstruse subjects, and yet could not tell how to improve the condition of the poorly cooked and still more poorly served bread and meat which they and their families were eating three times a day.[30]

Such passages are indicative of Washington's approach. He contrasted the material reality of poverty and untidiness to the idealistic illusion of success, created by familiarity with ancient languages. Such cultured activities clearly had not assisted black people in alleviating the real conditions of oppression. Moreover, such fancies had actually hindered the struggle against oppression. Delving into the culture of the dominant Western world merely gave the black elite the sensation of inclusion without the reality of equality.

The great danger of culture, then, was that it diverted needed energy away from seeking concrete practical changes. Whole black nations had slid into disrepute and disrepair because of the decadent diversionary emphasis by their leaders on culture. According to Washington:

> Haiti, Santo Domingo, and Liberia, although among the richest countries in natural resources in the world, are discouraging examples of what must happen to any people who lack industrial or technical training. It is said that in Liberia there are no wagons, wheelbarrows, or public roads, showing very plainly that there is a painful absence of public spirit and thrift. What is true of Liberia is also true in a measure of the republics of Haiti and Santo Domingo.[31]

In these black republics, the elite, deflected from doing real work because of their non-utilitarian European education, had rendered themselves useless for the primary task of constructing economically independent nations. Haiti, said Washington with scorn, "has to send abroad even to secure engineers . . . for her bridges and other work requiring technical knowledge and skill."[32] Without the development of really needed industrial and scientific education, these black republics were at the mercy of more powerful nations, to whom they had to turn for even the most basic technical assistance.

Washington could explain why cultural activity was so impractical. The engineer constructs a bridge within the secure framework of the laws of physics; the agronomist can predict the growth of seeds under specific conditions. In contrast, said Washington, literature, poetry, painting, and much of philosophical speculation were not subject to such precise requirements. Rather, their understandings tended toward a certain vagueness, an anti-rationality. Poetry and painting smacked of emotionalism and sensation, which were inimical to cool-headed thought.

In mathematics and in the physical sciences we can lay
down definite hard-and-fast rules, can be sure that a certain thing will be true tomorrow because it was true five
hundred years ago. . . . The higher one ascends, the further he gets away from the material and the more nearly
he approaches the intellectual and spiritual life, the more
uncertainty surrounds him.[33]

To be sure, Washington cautioned that "in the evolution of the races it is hardly possible to be guided by or
to reckon by mathematical rules."[34] Significantly, however,
he believed in the precision of the physical sciences and
mathematics against the "uncertainty" of "intellectual and
spiritual life." If science and mathematics could not provide
the ultimate and total guidance for a people, neither could
that people find guidance in an imprecise and emotional
view of the world. Racial unity could not simply be a matter
of ideals, of poems and pictures. It would be necessary to
"materialize [the] race."[35] That materialization would initially take place through the methods of the sciences and
mathematics. Just as a machine could be precision-built
through an understanding of physics, so could black people
begin to create themselves as an advancing and progressive
race:

When you say that an engine is a Corliss engine, people
understand that that engine is a perfect piece of mechanical work,—perfect as far as human skill can make it
perfect. And so with a race. You cannot keep back very
long a race that has the reputation for doing perfect work
in everything it undertakes.[36]

For Washington, cultural activity was marred by impreci-
sion; it lacked the more accurate analyses of the sciences
and the clarity of mathematics. A race that lacked scientists
and engineers lacked the very people necessary to construct
the foundations of racial progress. As the examples of Haiti,
Santo Domingo, and Liberia seemed to suggest to Washington, the absence of a trained cadre of scientists and engineers resulted in unnecessary decay, even when there were
abundant natural resources. A poet could not construct a
railroad, and railroads were necessary for economic free-

dom. To the degree that the physical sciences were more engaged in the material world, they were constantly being tested against its reality and so progressed. In contrast the humanities, further removed from the material world, were not tested against reality and did not progress.

Because racism was emotionally based, only the precision and cool rationality of the sciences could counteract it. It was necessary for any race to have engineers, scientists, and economists. But for black people, confronted by a nightmarish emotion-ridden form of thought, it was doubly necessary to align themselves with the rational capitalist emergence. If racism was sentiment, then the sentiment of literature not only was insufficient but it was cut from the same cloth as racism. Passion could not fight passion. A more fundamental materialist counterattack was called for.

This is the heart of Washington's critique of culture. For him, culture was in one important way an equivalent to racism. Washington saw both as modes of thought that emphasized emotion and sensation; both presented warped perspectives that negatively shaped action. Although they were losing money, racist businessmen continued in their racist ways. Although they were living in poverty, certain black people persisted in deluding themselves with a false environment of culture. Neither of these two ways of viewing the world accurately reflected the true situation; consequently, their users were unable to transform a setting that was fundamentally damaging to them. At most, these ways of viewing the world gave the sensation of power and success, but not the substance. Racists believed that they were actually protecting the white race, and classically educated black intellectuals believed that by wearing stylish clothes and quoting Plato, they had actually succeeded in escaping from racial oppression. All a mirage, thought Washington, a shivering image conjured up by a desire run amok, by passion without reason.

Washington detected, however, a fundamental difference between the irrationality of racism and the irrationality of culture. Racism was evil: it never could serve any good. Culture, however, was not fundamentally wrong. Its retrograde influence was more the result of a wrong-headed interpretation of the historic moment than an internal defect. The problem was that material change had by necessity to come before major intellectual artistic creativity. For culture to be shucked of its negative qualities, it would have to be "materialized." As a mode of thought, it would have to rest upon a material foundation. The first generations of black pioneers, carving out a new land after the barbaric slave age, could not be concerned with cultural amenities. But later generations, standing on the firm material foundation laid down by their elders, would be able to partake of culture. Their positive artistic achievements would flow easily and naturally from the changed conditions created by their more precise and scientific forebears:

> During the first fifty or one hundred years of the life of any people are not the economic occupations given the greater attention? If this generation will lay the material foundation, it will be the quickest and surest way for the succeeding generation to succeed in the cultivation of the fine arts, and to surround itself even with some of the luxuries of life, if desired.[37]

If literature and the arts were to grow from the base of economic power, they would reflect the achievements of the liberated people instead of being the domain of a detached privileged elite.

Washington's basic position is fundamentally materialistic. He argues that all thought and activity are ultimately derived from the material base of social existence. The material base of social existence is that mode of production that characterizes a society. Activities such as science and technology directly and clearly express this material foundation of social life. Because they are applied to the material world in a direct way, they are generally accurate expressions of it. Economic activity, because of its close dependence on science, technology, and mathematics, is similarly close to the material reality of society.

Some activities, however, reverse the real order of things and make images of the world more important than the world itself. Cultural activity, says Washington, tends in this direction. The poem that speaks glowingly of beauty in the midst of oppression, that gives its reader the sensation of escape from harsh realities, is such an activity. In this reversed consciousness of the world, ideas are seen as transcendent. That is, the ideas of poetry, art, and literature have no grounded material origin and therefore seem universal and outside of particular concrete circumstances of people's lives.

But, Washington argues, no ideas exist outside their particular immediate circumstances. Indeed, the very striving for transcendence through culture indicates the real subjugated state of the black elite. As religion was for Marx the opiate of the people, "culture" for Washington is the cry of a distressed people. It is their recoil from oppression. Their desperate attempt to emulate the culture of the oppressors indicates their real lack of economic power. Thus culture, like Marx's religion, reflects subordination and suffering. Culture gives the sensation of escape without the substance of freedom.

Consequently, for Washington the striving after culture contributes to the very condition from which people feel such deep need to escape. By encouraging people to avoid head-on confrontation with the real problem of the race's economic inferiority, culture diverts people's energies from necessary and effective action. Only when black people had freed themselves from oppression by their own material success would they be in a position to sustain the positive luxury of culture.

Booker T. Washington is seldom viewed as one who emphasized Afro-American culture as we understand that term today. He was mostly contemptuous of Africa and ruthless in his assertion that folkways had to be superseded by modern science. Yet there are important implications beneath the surface of his critique of culture and his argument that future generations will produce their own art and literature. Although Washington did not talk explicitly about the culture of the black nation, we find in his work the notion of a *grounded* literature and art. A grounded body of art and literature would be connected to the real world of the people and would no longer divert and delude.

At best, however, a grounded culture would provide spiritual and intellectual dimensions. It would remain impractical. There is no suggestion in Washington's writings that literature and the arts would become as precise and as practically useful as the sciences. They would just become somewhat more connected and therefore less dangerous.

By implication, Washington's argument contains an embryonic critique of the dominance of Western culture. Insofar as science and technology involve universal techniques and universal conditions, they are, whatever their origins, not confined to any one people. Similarly, economic activity lacks sentiment and is not the domain of any one people. Profit knows neither friends nor enemies. Washington, in effect, attempts to extract from the West its science, technology, and business, while urging immediate rejection of Western literature and art. Although he does not urge that rejection on the basis of the "Westernness" of culture, the culture that he calls illusory and dangerous is Western. In contrast, a bridge, a tractor, a factory are neither white, black, or Asiatic; they are neutral, available to any people who have the intelligence and courage to take them over.

For Washington, oppression had to be fought in the most concrete ways possible. Culture, as illusion, was hindering that fight. There were some, like Du Bois, who found Washington's claim to practicality and concreteness itself an illusion. But the content of Washington's argument was aimed against an elite that separated itself from the people through its illusion of cultured refinement. For Washington the imperative was clear—seize control of economic power and all else would follow. He proclaimed: "The study of art that does not result in making the strong less willing to oppress the weak means little."[38] On that hook Washington hung his critique of culture and his program for economic development.

W. E. B. Du Bois Constructs a High Culture of Resistance

In the early 1900s, W. E. B. Du Bois took a position that in key ways clashed with that of Booker T. Washington. Their differences cannot be categorized simply as a fight between a "radical" Du Bois and a "conservative" Washington.

The two apparent opponents actually held some important conceptual elements in common. No less than Washington, Du Bois wrestled with the contradiction between the appearance and reality of progress. He was painfully aware of the terrible price paid in human subjugation and misery to make that progress possible. His recognition of this contradiction led him to view racism as an integral part of capitalism and to see culture as autonomous and positive.

Was Western civilization to be equated with progress? Du Bois thought not, but his rejection of that equation was complex. He was highly enthusiastic about the advances made through science, yet he was outraged by the destruction of whole societies in the name of profit. Under the banner of "civilization," he observed, great evils had been and were being performed. Du Bois sought to simultaneously extract the positive elements of human development from the Western world and to expose the corrupt and corrupting understructure of that world. His work displays an intricate network of themes, sometimes praising, sometimes damning "civilization."

In his use of the term "principles of civilization," Du Bois made a vital distinction between the principles and the practice of "civilization." Referring to the World War, Du Bois noted, "to-day civilized nations are fighting like mad dogs over the right to own and exploit these darker peoples."[39] Du Bois saw the West's use of "brute force" against the "weak and the innocent" as barbaric. Civilization did not necessarily result in progress. In modern times it led to war and murder, slavery and debauchery. It was not the uncivilized "native" who was the barbarian. Du Bois, however, did not equate civilization and barbarism on the basis of such a pastoral argument. Modern civilization, he argued, had historically demonstrated that its barbarism was fundamental and internal, not simply a product of contact with more innocent peoples. Its acts were not those of madmen; on the contrary, said Du Bois, they were parts of plans carefully laid out by the captains of industry and by their political servants. Irrationality was not the source of corruption. The source was the cold and calculated lust for gain that had soiled the heart of civilized life. In his still pertinent work,

"The African Roots of the War," Du Bois traced the economic force behind the colonization and dismemberment of
Africa. The First World War, he declared, was

> the result of jealousies engendered by the recent rise of
> armed national associations of labor and capital whose
> aim is the exploitation of the wealth of the world outside
> the European circle of nations. These associations, grown
> jealous and suspicious at the division of the spoils of trade-
> empires, are fighting to enlarge their respective shares;
> they look for expansion, not in Europe but in Asia, and
> particularly in Africa.[40]

This profit-driven expansion into Asia and Africa could take
place only with the cooperation of white European workers.
Without that cooperation, imperial expansion would be impossible. Two years before Lenin's description of the co-
optation of European workers, Du Bois wrote:

> The difficulties of this imperial movement are internal as
> well as external. Successful aggression in economic ex-
> pansion calls for a close union between capital and labor
> at home. Now the rising demands of the white laborer,
> not simply for wages but for conditions of work and a voice
> in the conduct of industry, make industrial peace diffi-
> cult. The working men have been appeased by all sorts
> of essays in state socialism, on the one hand and on the
> other hand by public threats of competition by colored
> labor. . . . In addition to these national war-engendering
> jealousies there is a more subtle movement arising from
> the attempt to unite labor and capital in worldwide free-
> booting. Democracy in economic organizations, while an
> acknowledged ideal, is today working itself out by admit-
> ting to a share of the spoils of capital only the aristocracy
> of labor.[41]

Thus, argued Du Bois, capitalism entangled an important
element of the white labor force in assumptions of racial
superiority as a means of securing the European advance
across the face of the globe. Racism, in its pervasiveness,
was not confined to a few malcontents, nor was it confined
to the captains of industry. The "most advanced workers,"
hand-in-hand with the Rockefellers and Carnegies, were

using their Europeanness, their whiteness, as an important rationale for their "worldwide freebooting."

There was reason to believe that this co-optation of white labor could not be a complete success. Du Bois noted that it was the "aristocracy of labor" that was being so successfully incorporated. The others, "ignorant, unskilled, and restless still form a large threatening, and, to a growing extent, revolutionary group in advanced countries."[42] Between this group and the peoples of color of the world there might be forged a unity that would undercut the ignominious alliance between capitalists and white workers.

> War will come from the revolutionary revolt of the lowest workers. The greater the international jealousies, the greater the corresponding costs of armament and the more difficult to fulfill the promises of industrial democracy in advanced countries. Finally, the colored people will not always submit passively to foreign domination.[43]

Nonetheless, the association of whites with capitalism would essentially make this war one between the oppressed peoples of color and their white capitalist-labor rulers. Colored people were "going to fight and the War of the Color Line will outdo in savage inhumanity any war this world has yet seen. For colored folk have much to remember and they will not forget."[44] The war against white domination would of historic necessity be a war against capitalism.

For Du Bois, the world war then raging was not the work of men run amok. "This is not Europe gone mad, this is not aberration nor insanity, this is Europe,"[45] he pointed out. In every way, in every manipulation of the muscles and the brains of the oppressed, Western civilization had demonstrated its unfeeling nature. White rulers were willing and increasingly able to employ the most terrible methods for extracting profit from the sweating backs of "wogs," "coolies," and "niggers." When King Leopold's agents cut off black hands, they were not inflicting a peculiar punishment; such actions were central to the rise of imperialism. Whites have nothing to tell the peoples of color about being savage and primitive, proclaimed Du Bois, when they themselves have behaved like animals in order to fill their pockets.

If barbarism was intrinsic to the expansion of the Western world then it followed, for Du Bois, that some means of containing and reshaping that world was absolutely necessary.

In equating civilization with barbarism, Du Bois further argued that such cold calculation had taken a mechanistic form. Rational thought had become subordinated to the task of building more efficient machines—both in the sense of actual machines for industry and also in the sense of machine-like societies. In either manifestation, social or concrete, the machine had no love, no feelings. Mechanistic, task-oriented thought was the form of consciousness that kept such machinery running. The consequences of this mechanization of thought were devastating, said Du Bois.

But Du Bois's was no romantic reaction against science and technology. Hope was not to be found in an idyllic, pastoral past, and certainly, for Du Bois, it was not to be found in the "backward civilization" of the rural South. The solution was to seize control of the social-physical machine. Rather than encouraging modes of thought that helped the "armored might" of the world to run more smoothly, we should, said Du Bois, be creating forms of thought superior to the mechanical ways of conception:

> Anyone who suggests by sneering at books and "literary courses" that the great heritage of human thought ought to be displaced simply for the reason of teaching the technique of modern industry is pitifully wrong and if the comparison must be made, more wrong than the man who would sacrifice modern technology to the heritage of ancient thought.[46]

Every effort must be made, said Du Bois, to override the mechanical with a more humanistic view of the world, a view that could better direct the processes of industrial development than the narrow, self-serving technological philosophies of the day. There were, after all, no "mere mechanical problems":[47]

> Must industry rule men or may men rule industry. . . . We must spread that sympathy and intelligence which tolerates the widest individual freedom despite the necessary public control, we must learn to select for public

office ability rather than mere affability. We must stand ready to defer to knowledge and science and judge by results rather than by method, and finally we must face the fact that the final distribution of goods—the question of wages and income is not a mere mechanical problem and calls for grave public human judgment and not secrecy and closed doors.[48]

The mode of thought that would save the day, the intellectual frame for the necessary "ethical" and "public human judgment," was to be sought in basic universal principles. While Du Bois did not hearken back to a mythic rural past, he believed in the existence of an immutable and universal understanding of the world, an understanding that had been slowly and painfully constructed by great minds. This was the "heritage of ancient thought"—not simply a pile of dusty tomes but a key to understanding the human condition. Du Bois cited works from Plato to Josiah Royce and Rabindrinath Tagore as illustrations of the existence of universal principles of human conduct. The common message, Du Bois suggested, was the superiority of thought over matter; of the significance of the ethical over the narrowly practical; of the dominance of the spiritual over the mundane. He quoted approvingly from Josiah Royce: "Intellectual freedom means liberation from superstition and all the primitive manifestations of mental enslavement. The universal achieves the mastery over one's self."[49] And in Tagore, Du Bois found an example of one spiritually guided intellect in battle with materialism and greed. Du Bois published an excerpt from Tagore in the *Crisis*:

> In Europe we have seen noble hearts who have ever stood up for the rights of man, irrespective of color and creed; and who have braved calumny and insult from their own people in fighting for humanity's cause and raising their voices against the mad orgies of militarism, against the rage for brutal retaliation or rapacity that sometimes takes possession of whole people, who are always ready to make reparation for wrongs done in the past by their own nations and vainly attempt to stem the tide of cowardly injustice that flows unchecked because the resistance is weak. . . .[50]

Such thinkers and such thought, said Du Bois, were the products of civilization. More precisely, they were examples of a dimension of civilization that had not been destroyed, and could not be destroyed, by its more materialistic side. For Du Bois the essence of this dimension was a synthesis of the rational with the equally real and important strivings of the heart and the spirit. In this vein, the true science created by civilization involved a basic search for truth:

> Students must be careful to insist that science as such—be it physics, chemistry, psychology, or sociology—has but one simple aim, the discovery of truth. Its results lie open for the use of all men, merchants, physicians, men of letters, and philanthropists, but the aim of science itself is simple truth.[51]

This was the basic and general mission of science. Any narrower reading of that mission was bound to failure:

> Any attempt to give it [science] a double aim, to make social reform the immediate instead of the mediate object of a search for truth will inevitably tend to defeat both objects.[52]

Here Du Bois accepted the importance of science but attempted to deny the use of science to the technocrats. Any effort to make practical use of science would lose sight of the search for truth and so become, by implication, something other than science.

That a narrower technical or mechanical view of science was illusory and counterproductive was clear to Du Bois from his own experience:

> I became widely acquainted with the real conditions of my people. I realized the terrific odds which faced them. From captious criticism I changed to cold science, then to hot indignant defense. I saw the race hatred of the whites, naked and unashamed. I held back more hardly each day the mounting indignation against injustice and misrepresentation. I was faced with the awful paradox of death and birth—in fine, I emerged a man scarred, partially disillusioned, and yet grim with determination.[53]

The attempt to apply science directly against oppression could only result in a "cold science" that had little to say about "injustice." Science had its usefulness but only in a profound sense of the requirement that humankind search for truth. The truth, in its turn, involved more than the creation of machines; it also involved hot indignation against oppression. Tagore, then, was more a "scientist" than was the mere fiddler with test tubes or the builder of bridges.

The machinery of capitalism could be controlled, could be conquered, but only through a combination of mind and spirit. The result would be, not the destruction of that machinery, but rather its humanization, its "democratization," and hence its revolutionary transformation. It would become a controlled rather than a determining element in the world. An ethical machinery was possible:

> And we serve first for the sake of serving—to develop our own powers, gain the mastery of this human machine, and come to the broadest, deepest, self-realization.[54]

Out of this general control over the mechanistic society would come more specific programmtic steps of improvement and advancement:

> These steps are in many cases clear: the careful steady increase of public democratic ownership of industry, beginning with the simplest type of public utilities and monopolies, and extending gradually as we learn the way the use of taxation to limit inheritance and to take the unearned increment for public use beginning (but not ending) with a "single tax" on monopolized land values; the training of the public in business technique by cooperation in buying and selling, and in industrial technique by the shop committee and manufacturing guild.[55]

But always the guiding star for such specific proposals for reform was a transcendent ethic by which humans should live. The specific programs could not be the result simply of technocratic schedule making:

> But beyond all this must come the Spirit—the Will to Human Brotherhood of all Colors, Races and Creeds; the Wanting of the Wants of All. . . .[56]

Du Bois moved to expose the readers of *The Crisis* to the significance of ethical feeling as a means for understanding the world. In one issue, he reprinted a portion of John Ruskin's critique of Turner's painting, "The Slave Ship":

> I think the noblest sea that Turner has ever painted, and if so, the noblest ever painted by man, is that of the "Slave Ship." . . . Purple and blue, the lurid lighting of the sea, its thin masts written upon the sky in lines of blood, girded with condemnation in that fearful hue which signs the sky with horror, and mixes its flaming flood with the sunlight, and shadows of the hollow breakers are cast up.[57]

This imagery supported Du Bois's understanding of science and of the principles of civilization. Slavery, for example, had a rational base in capitalist expansion. That base had to be analyzed and understood as Du Bois had done so well in "The African Roots of the War." But understanding could not stop with such analysis. Turner's painting did not depict economic facts; the slave ship was portrayed as *guilty* of immorality, it was surrounded by "lurid lighting" to fit its sinful mission, and "lines of blood" flowed round it. Such description and sensation were the stuff of which a "grim determination" was constructed. For Du Bois, an all-embracing approach that combined economic analysis with "hot indignation" was essential. Any attempt to separate out science and use it in more constricted ways in hopes of ending oppression was doomed to failure. In sum, for Du Bois, a fundamental solution to the barbarism of machine-based civilization had to include the liberation of consciousness. The subservience of ethics to narrow mechanistic goals and to financial gain had to be overturned.

Du Bois's condemnation of civilization was an act of great faith in the potential of a more humanistic modern society. Had not great ideals been discovered by thinkers such as Royce and made vivid by artists such as Turner? The difficulty lay in the isolation of such people. Their struggle need not be in vain, thought Du Bois, but the battleground had to be clearly understood. The primary battles would take place as a form of philosophical revolution. The dominance of materialism, which emphasized the narrow interpretation of science as technique rather than truth and which reduced thought to machinery, would have to be usurped by a broad and critically humanistic view of the world. Real social change, such as the democratic ownership of industry, would follow from a radical transformation of consciousness among a revolutionary group of thinkers. Through "culture" —seen by Du Bois as ethically driven intellectual and artistic activity—a vanguard of warrior intellectuals, purged of the base materialism infecting the rest of society, would emerge to lead the battle against oppression.

Du Bois did not view Booker T. Washington simply as an accommodationist, as an apologist for the status quo. More fundamentally, Du Bois attacked Washington's assertion that oppression arose from the irrationality of racism and that capitalism was the saving grace. Washington looked on the South as a backward isolate, a rotting, sinking ship, that would be dissolved in a sea of progressive and mighty currents. The South, surrounded by capitalism, would be overwhelmed and transformed. Washington called black people to form a clear and conscious alliance with those forces of change that were about to overwhelm the South. He saw the black population as a fifth column that would open the way to the armies of progressive capitalism.

Du Bois took another view of the battle. He identified capitalism as the problem, arguing that racism functioned as an instrument of capitalist expansion across the world. Racism, rather than being an aberration, was a politically functional mode of thought that infiltrated almost all aspects of life. For Du Bois, the black response to such pervasive and corrupting oppression had to be a thoughtful retreat. What was desperately needed was a free territory within which to develop an effective resistance. From such a stronghold, the resisters could attack the dense concentration of oppression, slowly and patiently spreading the world of resistance, rebellion, and revolution.

Du Bois did not see this free territory as an actual piece of land. There was no place physically free from the power of capitalism. He did feel that the cities of the North offered more freedom of movement than did the rural South. While he expected more progressive change to take place in the urban North because it offered more freedom of movement, he did not paint a romantic picture of the liberated northern city. Because capitalism was for him the fundamental source

of racist brutality, he could not visualize the industrial cities
as the refuge for black resistance.

Nor did Du Bois think of Africa as a land of refuge. His
rejection of Africa was multifaceted, but the substance of
his rejection of Africa as a geographical refuge for black
Americans lay in his sense of their Americanness. Black
people in the United States, said Du Bois, were creations
of the New World; this was their homeland: "There are
today no truer exponents of the pure human spirit of the
Declaration of Independence than the American Negroes;
there is no true American music but the wild sweet melodies
of the Negro slave."[58]

There were, then, no places of actual physical refuge.
Black Americans could not congregate to plan the overthrow
of their enemies as did European émigrés in the shadowy
corners of friendly cities. The locations of black resistance
could not be physical and territorial; they would have to be
mental and spiritual. The means to develop these strong-
holds of the mind and the spirit was to be found in culture.

By culture, Du Bois meant a fundamentally independent way of thought. Culture—art, literature, philosophy,
and religion—could move independently of its origins. For
example: "Egyptian culture, however, gradually conquered
Ethiopia where her armies could not, and Egyptian religion
and civil rule began to center in the darker kingdom."[59]
Moreover, "From the fifth to the second century B.C. we
find the wild Sudanese pressing in [on Egypt] from the
West and Greek culture from the East."[60] Similarly, Greek
culture conquered Rome even while Greece declined politically. Du Bois saw Egyptian and Greek culture as distinct
from the political or military structures of those lands; it was
a force that could move and exercise influence as a separate
phenomenon.

The very fact that we use the terms Egyptian and Greek
to describe those cultures indicates for Du Bois that art,
literature, and philosophy arise from a historic foundation.
Culture is to be identified initially with a people and a
given movement in history. But the peculiarity of culture,
unlike the actual administration of a nation, is that it can
exist autonomously as thought and so move beyond politi-

cal borders. In contrast to culture, political systems are tied intimately to power, which travels only through itself. To exercise political influence requires actual control. The exercise of cultural influence requires only an influential system of thought.

In this description of culture as autonomous thought, Du Bois laid the theoretical basis for his image of a spiritual-philosophical sanctuary from which a black vanguard would emerge. In his terms, culture could be a "kingdom" unto itself. Within that kingdom, an elite black group, imbued with critical humanistic qualities, would develop untrammeled by the corruption of civilization and purified against the materialism of capitalism:

> There is a small but growing number of black men emerging into spiritual freedom and becoming participators and freemen of the kingdom of culture around which it is so singularly difficult to set metes and bounds and who in art, science, and literature are making their modest but ineffaceable mark.[61]

Within the "kingdom of culture," the intellectual activities of art and literature, science and philosophy, could flourish and mature. The development of intellectual activity would have an overall "spiritual" effect. From this cultural cauldron would emerge a highly ethical and deeply analytical view of the world, a view that would be fundamentally opposed to the rampant materialism of capitalism as proposed by either its white or black proponents. But perhaps most important in Du Bois's sense of culture is his assertion that it was "singularly difficult to set metes and bounds" around the "kingdom of culture."

Du Bois asserted the autonomy of culture as the foundation for resistance to oppression. The oppressors were dominant economically, politically, and militarily, but their powers were incapable of controlling the intellect and the spirit. Culture, a separate, transcendent domain, could not be totally incorporated by the oppressors, even when they made the most determined efforts to do so. Thus despite the whites' claim that Plato and Shakespeare were evidence of Caucasian superiority, such creative figures in fact transcended whiteness even as they could not be confined to particular national and temporal boundaries. The worth of Shakespeare was not his Elizabethanness but his dramatic appeal to universal problems of human existence. His works were not white; they were human and so beyond the call of racism. In that vein Du Bois noted wryly:

> I sit with Shakespeare and he winces not. Across the color line I move arm in arm with Balzac and Dumas, where smiling men and welcoming women glide in gilded halls. From out of the caves of evening that swing between the strong-limbed earth and the tracery of the stars, I summon Aristotle and Aurelius and what soul I will, and they come all graciously with no scorn nor condescension. So, wed with Truth, I dwell above the Veil.[62]

To be sure, racists would make every effort to set limitations on culture. To some extent they would be successful, given the tremendous power at their disposal.

> But the facing of so vast a prejudice could not but bring the inevitable self-questioning, self-disparagement and lowering of ideals which ever accompany repression and breed in an atmosphere of contempt of hate. Whispering and portents come borne upon the four winds. Lo! we are diseased and dying, cried the dark hosts; we cannot write, our voting is vain; what need of education, since we must always cook and serve? And the Nation echoed and enforced this self-criticism, saying: Be content to be servants and nothing more; what need of higher culture for half-men?[63]

Yet culture cannot be completely suppressed, said Du Bois, because it involves ethical, intellectual elements that a materialistic society cannot completely incorporate.

It would be within the stronghold of culture that the black vanguard would develop its critical powers. Standing separate from the rest of society, the vanguard could better comprehend the total picture of oppression. The view from the stronghold would be one of greater *depth* and *breadth*: "The foundations of knowledge in this race, as in others, must be sunk deep in the college and university if we would build a solid permanent structure."[64]

Out of such depths would come a critical and broad view of the world. This view would incorporate just enough detachment from the hot core of oppression to allow for the development of a sustained and significant analysis. The inhabitants of this cultural stronghold would be "black men of broad culture, catholic tolerance and trained ability."[65] Du Bois was explicit about the contrast between the type of resistance that can be developed through culture and the illusion of political power that the Reconstruction years had foisted on black people: "A million black men started with renewed zeal to vote themselves into the kingdom. So the decade flew away, the revolution of 1876 came, and left the half-free serf weary, wondering but still inspired."[66]

The failure to achieve actual political power was forcing a new cultural direction:

Slowly but steadily in the following years, a new vision began gradually to replace the dream of political power —a powerful movement, the rise of another ideal to guide the unguided, another pillar of fire by night after a clouded day. It was the ideal of "book learning" the curiosity born of compulsory ignorance, to know and test the power of the capitalistic letters of the white man, the longing to know.[67]

In the face of actual political weakness, with significant power not being within reach, culture offered the only substantial basis for a preparatory action. The turn toward culture was, said Du Bois, a necessary and historically conditioned outcome of the failure of Reconstruction to liberate black people. With the economic and political domains in the hands of the oppressors, culture was the only means with which to resist. Culture offered a basis for a cadre of intellectuals to develop as leaders of future movements.

For Du Bois, it was crucial that black intellectuals escape the grip of the oppressive society. It was in the intellectual borderlands, in areas that were not so important to the oppressor as economics and politics, that Du Bois sought to establish the locus of resistance. There, the vanguard would learn to comprehend the world in a way not possible to those bent under the whips of the hated masters. Freed from the external struggle to survive, the vanguard would see clearly, broadly, and deeply. Of himself, Du Bois wrote:

> High in the tower, where I sit above the loud complaining of the human sea, I know many souls that toss and whirl and pass, but none there are that intrigue me more than the Souls of White Folk. Of them, I am singularly clairvoyant. I view them from unusual points of vantage.[68]

Du Bois took the peripherality of the black race, its segregation into the furthest corners of existence, and boldly transformed it into a positive location for revolution. Rather than being despised, the margin was accepted as the only point from which resistance could truly take place. Through culture, the vanguard would return to the world armed and purified—warriors of the spirit and the mind.

Washington, Du Bois, and Society

Now, let us make some comparisons of Washington with Du Bois. There are numerous important lines of convergence and divergence that simultaneously pull them apart and together. Washington, as I have suggested, had a contained view of racial oppression in the United States. The brutal system of control that was centered in the South, was, for him, irrational. The racism that could be found north of the Mason-Dixon line did not directly concern Washington because he considered the South to be the only area within which black people could truly advance. Southern racism, because it lacked any sustaining rational foundation, would give way before the historically grounded force of capitalism. Du Bois held the opposite. Racism for him was not a phenomenon to be overcome by economic power but rather was intimately a part of the entire imperialist advance of capitalism. From every street corner in every industrial city to the furthest rubber plantations and banana bottoms of Africa, Asia, and Latin America, capitalism was working its "wogs" and "coolies." Racism was the justification for that economic domination. Through racism, whole societies were being reduced to mere cogs in the global machine of capitalism. This development of capitalism at the expense of the colored peoples of the world was taking place in a lucid and conscious way as a fundamental part of the driven effort to increase profits. There was nothing insane about racism. It was functional.

It is not surprising that, given their different positions, the image of the machine would be positive for Washington and negative for Du Bois. For Washington, the more machine-like society became, the more free it would be from irrational emotion. For Du Bois, the machine represented the very inhumaneness of profit-driven capitalism. The less society was like a machine, the better off people would be.

These views of the source and nature of oppression coincide with quite different perspectives on culture. For Washington, confronting oppression required a cold profit-driven kind of thought that could challenge the emotionalism of the racists. Culture did nothing to help because culture itself appealed to sentiment, to feeling, to the ambiguous and the impractical. Worse, culture deluded the very elite that should have been playing the most important economic role into thinking it had power when in fact all it had was a dream. Oppression must be fought through cold capitalist rationality. Black people would be able to play an important role in the development of Southern capitalism only if they were prepared to think in practical, rational ways. Anything else was a waste of energy and a diversion of needed analysis.

For Du Bois, mechanical capitalist rationality was not a remedy for racism; racism was a tool employed by the capitalists in their drive toward ever greater gain. Science and technology, while inherently neutral, were easily bent by the powerful to their will. What was needed was a humanistic control of science and technology, but humanistic control could only take place in a fundamentally different form of consciousness that rejected capitalist profits and blind respect for science. Such consciousness could not develop, said Du Bois, in the very heart of capitalism. With the economic and political systems totally engaged in the advancement of industry, the only avenue for effective resistance leading to eventual revolutionary transformation was culture. Through the disciplined study of the great currents of humanistic thought, black thinkers would develop both the critical method and the critical theory needed to challenge and overcome the status quo.

Culture, being inherently autonomous and not subject to the same degree of control as economics and politics, was the natural domain for resistance. The great works of art and literature, by their very transcendent character, offered a platform for looking out over the battleground and comprehending it from a distance. Simultaneously, those great works demanded an ethical dimension that prevented them from being too detached and aloof. This was the culture of an engaged elite. Blazing forth with a system of thought, which was rigorously analytical and spiritually alive, this black vanguard group would strike back into the heartland of the oppressors and lift up their bound and suffering brethren.

Washington and Du Bois also had two quite different perspectives on the significance of art and literature. Washington contrasted fundamental issues such as economic change with superficial forms of thought such as racism, politics, and culture. All those forms of thought were epiphenomenal, lacking in substance. They ultimately had their source in the more basic conditions of the economic system. Du Bois shared with Washington a distrust of politics as superficial. Had not Reconstruction demonstrated the ineffectiveness of political forums for change? And, like Washington, Du Bois contrasted the superficiality of politics with something more profound. But for Du Bois, the something more profound was culture—the very form of thought that Washington saw as illusory. Further, Du Bois saw Washington's economics not as the ground for everything else but as a derivation and effect of consciousness. It was not through control of the more secondary economic system but through transformation of consciousness that change would occur. The economy, harnessed to a new humanistic way of thought, would be a different economy.

Washington and Du Bois thus both relied on images of depth and superficiality in their analysis of culture, economics, racism, and politics. They chose to locate these elements at quite different places on a scale measuring the basic and the superficial, however. Both interpreted the failure of Reconstruction as revealing the superficiality of electoral politics. Both sought a deeper, more substantial, level of action that would not so easily be destroyed. They differed in that Washington put the deeper level in the economy, Du Bois in culture.

But Washington and Du Bois fundamentally agreed that the real strategic necessity was to organize an elite around a central point of struggle from which all else would flow. Their intense conflict with one another developed from this shared Vanguard perspective rather than from fundamental differences. It was precisely because each of them accepted the basic notion that there should be one leading group, one domain of struggle, and one blueprint for action, that they could not accept each other's variations.

3

The Messenger and *The New Negro*

Although Du Bois was a worldly, well-traveled person, and Washington had observed conditions first-hand in Europe, their formulations of the Vanguard perspective largely emerged from confrontation with the agrarian problems of Afro-Americans. After all, over 90 percent of the black population was concentrated in the rural South at the turn of the century. The United States had not yet become a major industrial nation.

By the 1920s much of this environment had been altered. Under the impetus of the war, the United States had increased its industrial capacity, attracting millions of black people from the rural south to the urban north. Large concentrations of black people were forming in cities like Pittsburgh, Detroit, and Chicago. Meanwhile, technological developments had improved communication and transportation. The impact of the Russian Revolution was being felt far and wide. The European conquest of all Africa, excepting tiny Liberia and isolated Ethiopia, had been essentially completed. There was a surge in colonialism alongside the stirrings of anti-colonial movements. There was revolution and increased repression from fear of revolution.

In this changed and ever more urbanized and global environment, black people in general became part of the accelerated cosmopolitan spirit of the times. Black American soldiers, who had fought in Europe alongside not only Europeans but colonial troops from around the world, and who had been treated with respect in France, returned with an outlook informed by war and contacts with other peoples. The capacity of black people to communicate both within the United States and among other black and colonized peoples improved with the general increased effectiveness of communication and transport technologies. For example, the *Chicago Defender* was read not just in that city but throughout the South. Similarly, the newspapers of the Universal Negro Improvement Association were printed in a number of languages and distributed throughout Africa, Europe, the Carribean, Central and South America, as well as the United States.

In this more cosmopolitan environment following "The Great War," there are two major illustrations of Vanguard perspective efforts to consolidate elite direction of the masses. One of these is the self-described "radical" socialist magazine, the *Messenger*. The other important example is the manifesto of the New York black literati, artists, and others, whose outlooks Alain Locke brought together in the 1925 work, *The New Negro*. The *Messenger* and *The New Negro* largely recapitulated the debate between Washington and Du Bois. The *Messenger* took an essentially materialistic view that emphasized economic power as the basis for all change, and *The New Negro* opted for an idealistic approach with an emphasis on culture and consciousness. Like the Washington-Du Bois debate, these two distinct positions were both rooted in the Vanguard perspective.

The Messenger

During the First World War, a number of black socialists began contributing articles to the newspaper, the *Messenger*, founded by A. Philip Randolph and Chandler Owen. The *Messenger* provided a unique forum for a wide variety of leftist writings within the New York black community. By examining this variety, we can uncover the key tendencies of Randolph's and Owen's approaches to the struggle for freedom. As editors they shaped the tone and content of the *Messenger*.

One striking tendency, running through important articles in the *Messenger*, is the direct use of the machine analogy for analyzing society. Not unlike Washington, the *Messenger* extolled the virtues of machine-like discipline in a progressive cause. Conversely, the *Messenger* criticized the political machinery of the Democratic and Republican parties and those, such as Du Bois, who on occasion urged support for those parties. From the *Messenger* perspective, supporters of the mainstream parties were little more than cogs carrying out mechanical duties of supporting the status quo. "Men do not own their own souls in legislatures. They are part of the machine, and they must move with the machine or else they will be crushed."[1] Consequently, argued *The Messenger*, a black Republican or a black Democrat could not act in the best interests of the black population. They owed their allegiance to the machine.

The socialist criticism of mechanical politics did not stop at that level. More fundamentally, the parties were themselves elements in the wider machinery of capitalism, serving powerful behind-the-scenes interests. The *Messenger* asserted, "These Republican and Democratic Parties are just vestigial capitalist tools. Neither white nor colored representatives of the old parties have any initiative, independence or freedom of action."[2] The danger of the two parties was not that they were machines but that they served as instruments for "real estate interests" and others. Subservience to the machine was in fact subservience to people of power and wealth. The mechanical allegiance of politicians was an instrument by which the capitalists controlled the elected representatives of the people.

Black people could expect no succor from black Republicans because their souls had been bought:

> If the Republican Party, which is supported by the real estate interests, nominates a Negro for the Assembly from a District in which Negroes are largely of the tenant class, who desire low rents, and the best services obtainable, and this Negro is elected to office, and a measure in the Legislature intended to abolish the law of dispossess

is raised, the Negro legislator in question undoubtedly would oppose this measure. Now, Why? The reason is simply this: A man will not oppose his benefactor. Since the Republican Party is controlled by Real Estate Interests, and the Real Estate interests benefit from the "law of dispossess," which gives them the power to eject tenants when they fail to pay their rents promptly, this Negro who is a nominee on the Republican ticket, could not, and would not oppose the "law of dispossess" which his benefactor—The Republican Party—is the beneficiary.[3]

For the *Messenger* the image of the social machine could be either negative or positive. The real issue was who controlled and shaped this machinery. When describing the Socialist party or the Bolsheviks, the *Messenger* employed the term "machine" in a more positive way. In his praise of the Russian Revolution, Randolph wrote:

It's all like a dream! In Russia one-hundred and eighty millions of peasants and workmen—disinherited, writhing under the ruthless heel of the Czar, for over three hundred years, awoke and revolted and drove their hateful oppressors from power. Here a New Crowd arose—the Bolshevi, and expropriated the expropriators. They fashioned and established a new social machinery—the soviet—to express the growing class consciousness of the teeming millions, disillusioned and disenchanted. They also chose new leaders—Lenin and Trotsky to invent and adopt new scientific methods of social control; to marshall, organize and direct the revolutionary forces in constructive channels to build a New Russia.[4]

Here the "new social machinery" directed by "new scientific methods of social control" becomes a positive emblem of profound and progressive change. The machinery of the Bolsheviks had what the Republican and Democratic parties could not have—"the energy and support of one-hundred and eighty million of peasants and workmen."[5] The implication was that the machinery of socialism ultimately is derived from the will of the people. Disciplined party organization, directed by new means of social control and emerging from the masses, becomes positive machinery.

Thus, the underlying tendency in the *Messenger* was not to criticize highly controlled party organization as such. The publication viewed social machinery as ultimately neutral and measured its value by who controlled it.

To the *Messenger*, the foundation of party machinery was the economic system. Those who controlled the economy controlled the actions of the parties. Moreover, those who controlled the economy controlled the fate of millions of people. The Great War raging in Europe was itself a product of conflict between competing capitalist centers:

> The industrial revolution has given the world labor saving machines. Labor saving machines have produced an economic surplus. Capitalists who control this surplus desire the highest return on their investments. The highest return may be secured in the undeveloped countries, Asia, Africa, and China. This then is the reason for capitalists using the government to secure economic spheres of influence in these countries. They want raw material. They want to sell the consumers goods, such as hats, shoes, etc. All countries are directly or indirectly fighting for these things.[6]

But the *Messenger* did not locate the source of war in economic considerations alone. Few die, suggested Randolph, so that more shoes may be sold in China or that more rubber may be extracted from Liberia. Rather:

> Economic and political factors are reinforced by psychological ones. . . . Each country has national slogans, shibboleths, rallying emotional symbols which rule the people by law of suggestibility. The flag is waved; a slogan is proclaimed, the people are agitated; they visualize the sacred hearth of their country violated by the ruthless feet of the foe and they fly to arms.[7]

This psychological response was essentially emotional and irrational. The response of people to slogans, to basic primordial images of the violation of the home, reflected the most primitive kinds of fears. But for Randolph, even this irrationality was far from being the primary cause of war. Rather, these primeval responses of attack and defense were brilliantly understood and manipulated by the capitalists in a most rational and calculated fashion:

> The slogan "Britannia rules the waves" stirs the hearts of the poverty stricken Briton, though he may not own a single foot of land in the whole empire. It creates prejudice against non-Britons. The Rothschilds, the Lansdownes and their like know its value to protect over-sea investments.[8]

The manipulation of emotion in the service of hidden rationality was not limited to warfare, argued the *Messenger*. The same model applied to the understanding of any racial oppression. The barbaric and brutal racism of the lynch mob, as abhorrent and beyond comprehension as it might seem—those white men, women, and children standing in a grinning mob over the charred remains of a black man's body—such acts were part of the wider picture of capitalist control. Both the lynch mob and the poor Englishman dying in Flanders to defend "Britannia" lacked awareness of the puppet's role they were playing. But despite their lack of consciousness of their own manipulation, scientifically trained minds were aware that all such "irrational" acts were serving certain functions in the capitalist system.

In his article "Private Property as a Pillar of Prejudice," W. A. Domingo laid out the *Messenger* perspective on the usefulness of racism:

> Nearly every manifestation of race prejudice in the South, Jim-Crowism, lynching, peonage and the farm lien system can be traced to material motives. Even the elaborate propaganda of Southern race prejudice in the North has an economic background, for it is the desire of the South that all America should acquiesce in its Bourbon determination to keep Negroes in an economic situation that makes it possible for their labor to be ruthlessly exploited.[9]

There were, said Domingo, the few who recognized the economic reasons for their claims of racial superiority— "that section of the white population which by origin, tradition, education and material advantages controls newspapers, writes magazine articles, monographs, books and plays." This mercantile-elite sector of the South, through its control over the instruments of information and knowledge, manipulated the "ignorant, deluded and degraded hill-billies" and "crackers."[10] For the *Messenger* writers, newspapers, the theater, churches, and schools were controlled by the capitalists, who would not hesitate to employ them as a means of maintaining division between black and white workers. For the capitalist, a depressed and servile black work force offered a constant check to unionization efforts by labor. Black people could be used as scabs to break strikes. Moreover, a controlled black work force was the backbone of production in commercial agriculture. The reinforcement of this domination over black workers was, said the *Messenger*, crucial to the expansion of capitalism. To the degree that organized labor accepted racist definitions of black people, they were playing into the hands of the capitalists. The result of such antagonisms was a labor movement fractured into racial camps and consequently unable to unite in resistance to factory owners. "The race riot," argued the *Messenger*, "was the most effective instrument" against the unity of black and white workers.[11]

Racism, then, was not simply an emotional phenomenon. But neither was racism rational, any more than was jingoistic patriotism. The genius of capitalism, suggested the *Messenger*, was the way in which it had managed to make use of highly irrational dimensions in human thought. Patriotism and racism, primordial in their senselessness, were subsumed as instruments. The rational made use of the peculiar features of the irrational.

For the *Messenger* writers, capitalism was a formidable and solidly entrenched enemy. Aside from its direct and often brutal control over the police and military apparatus of the state, a control that led to violent suppression of protest as well as to global conflict, the capitalists had learned how to manipulate the very emotions of the general population. This manipulation was crafty and subtle enough to beguile the scientifically untutored. Controlling consciousness and controlling the strong arms of law and order, the capitalists dominated not only the United States but the entire world.

What would it take to transform or to overturn this control? The *Messenger* response to this question took many forms, but at its core was a belief in revolutionary changes. These changes would have to be multi-dimensional: it would be necessary to seize control of the instruments of persuasion, such as newspapers and the theater. More fundamentally, there would have to be significant shifts in the social-economic organization of the working class. Ultimately, the entire structure of capitalism would have to be altered.

Black intellectual thought of the time emphasized evolutionary progress. Both Washington and Du Bois saw change as "progressive," both in the sense of a positive advancement and also in the sense of a more or less gradual transformation of existing conditions. The socialist writers of the *Messenger* saw the situation quite differently: they envisioned a sudden, violent, and cataclysmic social upheaval that would lift years of oppressive weight. Further, such change would not be isolated in one small pocket of the globe but would sweep in a raging conflagration across the earth.

Crucial to the development of this image of total global revolutionary change was the apparent success of the Bolshevik revolution. In *Messenger* thinking, the Russian Revolution was a symbol, not simply of what could be done, but of what had been done. References to the Bolsheviks figure prominently in the various issues of the *Messenger*. "In Russia," wrote Randolph, "the peasants have hurled their oppressors from power and the Soviet, the peoples' government stands defiant before the imperialist world."[12] This victory had occurred in the teeth of an infamous and powerful attempt to crush socialism. "Democracy has triumphed in Russia," wrote the *Messenger*, and its enemies were laid low:

> The Czarist minions and their capitalist supporters in France, Great Britain, the United States, Japan and about eighteen other countries, placed their money upon the wrong horse. They had not reckoned with the indomitable courage and the cold resolution born of the unconquerable love for liberty. They really believed that if they could corrupt the press the demand for Liberty

would fall. But in all their conclusions they were wrong. Their conclusions were fallacious because their premises were not true.[13]

So, the Bolshevik revolution had, said the *Messenger*, overcome two major elements in the structure of capitalist domination. It had undermined the control of consciousness by the media. Fradulent news stories could not dismiss the actual triumph of the oppressed. Even more important was the tremendous sense of achievement. Capitalism was not invincible. The most powerful nations in the world, with great armies and navies at their disposal, had been unable to defeat workers and peasants driven by an "unconquerable love for liberty."

An important part of the triumph in Russia, said the *Messenger*, was the subsequent attack on anti-Semitism. In his article "Did Bolshevism Stop Race Riots in Russia?" Domingo observed similarities between the condition of Russian Jews and Afro-Americans:

> Perhaps the greatest analogy between Russian and the United States can be found in the former's treatment of Jews and in the latter's treatment of Negroes. Under the autocratic Czar, Jews were treated in very much the same manner as Negroes are treated in the Democratic United States. They had no political rights, they were segregated within the Pale, and the avenues of sorrow, oppression and despair. Just as American Negroes had had their Atlanta, East St. Louis, Washington and Chicago, so had the Jews of Russia their Kisineff and other pogroms. Just as Negro loyalty in wars has proven futile as a deterrent or preventative of lynch law and oppression so did Jewish fealty to Russia prove non-effective in abating their persecution and suffering.[14]

But the Bolsheviks, Domingo asserted, had made determined efforts to halt the oppression of the despised minority:

> One of the first things the new government did was sternly to suppress and punish those of the old regime

who had retained the old psychology of race hatred if caught inciting the people to start pogroms—race riots— against Jews. After a few executions of lynchers and race rioters the Bolshevik government succeeded in making Soviet Russia unsafe for mobocrats, but safe for Jews and other oppressed minorities.[15]

In this way, argued the *Messenger*, racism, one of the main props of capitalist domination, had been brought down. Thus Bolsheviks had destroyed the instruments of oppression in the form of the news media and in the form of racism; they had also seized control of the state itself. They had uprooted the main structures of oppression, a victory accomplished through armed revolution.

As we have seen, for the *Messenger*, racism was irrational emotion harnessed by the capitalist machine. But emotion could contribute to revolution as well as to oppression. The anti-Semitic "blood lust" of the common Russian soldier, encouraged by "newspapers" and "priests," was defeated by "dogged and determined" revolutionaries "goaded on by the cries of emaciated children and the piteous appeals of women."[16] This imagery of the revolutionary is highly romantic; it is charged with sensation. Indignation at the suffering of loved ones (an emotion not too different from the patriot's enraged defense of the endangered homeland) became for the *Messenger* writers a fundamental source of revolutionary energy. The success of the Bolsheviks was attributed partly to their ability to harness the emotion of the oppressed. Significantly, the outrage of the oppressed had been contained by "the new social machinery" that had been developed through "new scientific methods of social control." These methods had been used to "marshall, organize and direct the revolutionary forces."[17]

The *Messenger* contended that the powerful forces of outrage and fear were particularly susceptible to manipulation by more rational minds. The capitalist encouraged racist emotion as a means of dividing the working class. The "scientific socialists" such as Lenin and Trotsky similarly were able to harness the "Promethean fires" of the peasantry, but for different purposes. When wisely and rationally directed by socialist objectives, the emotions of the Russian workers and peasants had been directed at the oppressors rather than at the scapegoat Jewish population.

The *Messenger* thus saw the ability to harness and direct basic emotions, and to oppose the capitalist direction of emotions, as crucial to revolutionary success. The machinery of an oppressive state could be overturned by another kind of machinery—that of the revolutionary party. The difference between these two mechanical structures was in the interests they served. The society of Russia under the Czar served the Czars, the landowners, and the capitalists. The machinery of the revolutionary society was derived from, and served the interests of the people. But the people's interests were not directly tied to the organization of the revolutionary party or state; rather, leaders like Lenin and Trotsky who initiated scientific analysis had provided direction. With the help of such leadership, the emotions and energies of the people were translated into rational strategy and tactics, both during and after the revolutionary victory. The machinery of the revolution needed its social technicians.

This view of the Bolshevik triumph as a combination of Promethean energy and dispassionate science was powerful for the *Messenger* writers. The impact of the Russian example was, however, even further enhanced by a sense of its global effects. The *Messenger* viewed the events in Russia as exemplary of a more widespread upheaval which was about to transform the world: "The times are pregnant with change. Nothing escapes the God of Metamorphosis. Even empires rise and fall. Kings are disposed, Kaisers exiled and Czars banished."[18] For Domingo it was clear that: "A new spirit is abroad in the world. Ancient wrongs and oppressions arc melting before the rising wrath of the masses of the entire world.[19]

The global quality of this "new spirit" was nothing less than the fusion of otherwise disparate peoples. Across racial, ethnic, and linguistic lines, the oppressed were joining in one great sweeping march against tyranny:

Subject races, small nationalities and oppressed workers are realizing their kinship. The white workers of Russia, the yellow coolies of Korea, the brown ryots of India and the black toilers of Africa, the West Indies and the United States are making similar demands upon their oppressors, although they and their masters in many instances are alike in race, color, language, and religion.[20]

It was not cultural affinity and linguistic ties that were paramount. What did it matter if the slave and the master spoke the same tongue? They were still slave and master. Rather: "Labor is the common denominator of the working of the world. Exploitation is the common denominator of the oppressed everywhere."[21]

Black people, then, would have to recognize that their lot was not peculiar to them. There were many other oppressed peoples. Similarly, the solution to oppression, which was the rising up of the world peoples, could not be restricted to one oppressed group. Black people were linked to the rising tide of liberation engulfing the globe. The *Messenger* emphasis was on the common denominator of exploited laborers rather than on exploited races.

In the first place the Negro is not the only race that is now being oppressed. Brown Hindu, Yellow Chinese and White Irishmen are equally, and in some instances more oppressed than Negroes. The worst oppressors are not all Caucasians. Among the worst oppressors are found the Japanese, a yellow nation. In the dim past Negroes were among the greatest oppressors in the world. The Egyptians who, according to the Bible, enslaved the Jews were a dark people of admitted Negro blood. Oppression is not racial . . . no particular race has absolutely clean hands.[22]

This passage gives us clearer sense of the *Messenger's* view of leadership for the exploited. Black people, it argued, were tied to the other subjugated workers of the world both by common oppression and by common struggle. This objective fact did not mean, however, that all black people recognized that commonality. Indeed, the problem, from the *Messenger* viewpoint, was that other black political activists and many in the black masses mistakenly viewed racial and not economic oppression as crucial. Consequently, it was imperative that those prescient and enlightened black activists who *did* comprehend the economic roots of struggle and oppression be in the forefront to lead the people in the right direction. This leading group was both a product of the world-wide commonality of the economically oppressed, and an interpreter of that commonality to the black population as well.

> Finally, the New Negro arrived upon the scene at the time of all other forward, progressive groups and movements—after the great world war. He is the product of the same world wide forces that have brought into being the great liberal and radical movements that are now seizing the reins of political, economic, and social power in all of the civilized countries of the world.[23]

Armed with their special knowledge of the "world-wide forces," the "New Negro" would lead the general black population to become active rather than passive participants in global change: "Yes, there is a New Negro, and it is he who will pilot the Negro through this terrible hour of storm and stress."[24] Notice here the important distinction between the terms "New Negro" and the "Negro." The New Negro is the leading group for the rest of the black population. It is tied to the population of its origin, yet, through its knowledge of the wider picture, the New Negro is also linked to broader developments of which the general black population knows little.

In addition to the Bolshevik example, a series of events in the United States gave support to the *Messenger* conviction that a global revolution was underway—a revolution in which black people would play an important role. Throughout the war years there had been a number of lynchings and mob attacks on black people. In 1917, the year the Bolsheviks came to power, a series of vicious pogroms against black people took place in a number of cities including Philadelphia and East St. Louis. In Houston, black soldiers who had been attacked by whites took to arms and fired on the city police station. The fighting that followed took thirty-nine lives. Thirteen of the black soldiers were later hanged by the army. No whites were punished. The East St. Louis battle resulted in the death of forty black people, as white mobs stalked the streets looking for victims. The violence in that city led one U.S. congressman to ask, "What chance on earth has a poor, innocent Negro in a place like this?"[25]

But it was not the murder of "poor innocent Negroes" that attracted the attention of the *Messenger*. Rather, it was examples of black resistance. William Colson pointed out that thousands of black soldiers returning from the war, "now possess weapons to demonstrate if need be their legal right to self-defense. . . ."[26] The *Messenger* noted that in Chicago resistance to the mob had been at least partially successful. Black homes in the city had been bombed. No arrests had been made. The whites "growing bolder because of the seeming docility of the Negro and the laxity of authorities made open threats to mob Negroes on the 4th of July in Washington Park." The response by black people was immediate. "Colored men taking precautions quietly secured pistols, Winchesters, Springfield rifles and even machine-guns from 'God knows where.'"[27] Their precautions were not in vain. A black youth, swimming in Lake Michigan was blown into the white section of a beach and was immediately stoned to death. Black people on the beach demanded that the police act. They refused. Mobs of whites formed and were joined by the police, who seemed to be allies of the lynchers rather than guardians of the peace.

Throughout the black belt ghetto of Chicago, black men and women prepared to defend themselves.

The white mobs surged. Black men charged, defying, killing, and wounding policemen and civilians. Sunday, Monday, and Tuesday nights they killed two whites to their one of Negroes. At 35th, 39th, 37th, 47th, and 51st streets, the whites tried to come through in mass formation, but they were driven back in great losses.

White auto squads from the loop in one instance carrying a machine gun made flank movements through this belt but the machine-gun man was killed and the gun taken.[28]

Because of the black resistance, when the state militia was finally called, it acted cautiously and did not join in with the white mobs. Chicago was hardly Moscow. But for the *Messenger* writers, the sight of armed black resistance to lynch mobs seemed part of the world-wide resistance by the oppressed. And as in Russia, despite the acquiescence of the police, despite the always looming threat of the army, and despite the control of the media, by their act of resistance black people had taken control of the situation and turned it into a victory. Within this image of heroic struggle is another element. The black population of Chicago faced a seething sea of "race hatred" and "race madness,"[29] an irrational mob, acting unconsciously in the service of divide-and-rule-capitalism. Their response to the mob was not simply more irrationality. Rather, the *Messenger* noted, they were thoughtful and deliberate in their defense. Rationality in control of the emotion, emotion fueling the rational—this was the heart of the Chicago resistance. Similar forms of resistance had taken place elsewhere, the *Messenger* pointed out. In each case the forces of oppression had been forced to retreat. Cossacks and lynch mobs all dissipated before an outraged and determined people.

Nonetheless for black people, indeed for working people, to achieve a revolutionary change in the United States would require a more complete development of this heady mix of emotion and rationality. The *Messenger* saw preparing the ground for revolutionary change as partly a problem of changing consciousness or "philosophy," and partly a problem of action, including purposeful violence. The problem of consciousness and its relationship to action thus occupied much of the *Messenger's* analysis.

For the *Messenger* socialists, consciousness was profoundly shaped by the economic nature of society. As we have seen, the *Messenger* writers were alert to the ways in which consciousness was manipulated through emotion and through newspapers, schools, and churches. Those who control the economic system, argued the *Messenger*, make constant and clever use of these instruments to justify and sustain their positions of control. Capitalists were making every effort to turn black people away from the critical analysis and actions offered by socialism while keeping black and white workers separated through the spectre of racism:

> The leading capitalist of the country artfully and persistently prosecuted an insidious campaign of propaganda among Negroes, through the press, pulpit, and school, with a view to making them fire-proof to all liberal and democratic opinions. The jim-crow Negro censorship either withholds from or misrepresents the radical movements through the world, to the Negro.[30]

The consequences of such manipulation, said the *Messenger*, was the debilitation of the socialist movement:

> When one is uninformed of the nature of a movement he is disinclined to entertain it, and when one is misinformed concerning the objects and aims of a movement, he is inclined to oppose it. Hence through the ignorance or error the opposition of the Negro to the very movements which are calculated to achieve his economic political emancipation, is being effected by hand-picked Negro leaders—and the plutocratic interests of this country.[31]

The attack on this manipulation would have to be twofold, said the *Messenger*. Only by seizing control of important points in the economic system could black workers change their subordinate position. The problem before black workers could not be met by a legalistic struggle against segregationist laws nor by improvements in the schools. "The chief need of the Negro," wrote the editors, "is the organization of his industrial power."[32] This statement reflected the belief that black workers were a crucial part of the working class. Their primary task, from which all else would flow, was to organize effectively at all places of work. Through such organization, black workers could, along with white workers, employ the highly efficient weapon of the strike. But strikes were not important in big industry and agriculture alone. By organizing in all forms of jobs, workers could come to exercise greater control over their work conditions. Those who worked in the arts were no exception. The creative potential of the black artist could only be realized under economically-liberated conditions. The *Messenger* took this position on the grounds that the art and literary worlds were businesses and were controlled by businessmen who exploited the artist and the writer just as "any other employer will exploit a working man."[33] The question of art was the question of economic control. In its appeal to black artists, the *Messenger* argued, "The Negro actor needs a union with which to get longterm contracts from the theatrical management. Otherwise your job may depend upon the whims and caprices of some petty pilfering profiteer."[34]

Under capitalism creativity is stifled, if it is not still-born. With a socialist union organization, however, the artist would be liberated from the demands of making profit for others and would be able to engage in truly creative activity. As a worker, the artist was in need of, and capable of forming, the same type of organization as were other workers. The producers of culture could be forged into unions and cooperatives. They could strike. They could ultimately seize control of their work places. Through such control, they would be able to transform their creativity, freeing it from the oppressive effect of capitalist commercialism.

This social-economic reorganization of culture would involve a more "scientific" form of expression. As the culture makers became more integrated through unions and co-operatives into the progressive machinery of socialism, their work would have to become more "objective" and "practical," more analytical and observant of the real world. In a word, art and literature would have to become naturalistic to serve in the construction of socialist society. "Naturalism" was, consequently, a powerful idiom for the transforming of culture. The naturalistic painter or writer would come to resemble the scientific observer.

The flights of passion, which the *Messenger* writers discerned in Du Bois's writing, would be tightly controlled.

Naturalism was seen as an important artistic format through which socialism would coordinate the attack against the perceived overwrought emotion endemic in art and literature. Great art was defined as that art which most precisely and explicitly reduced the artist to the role of acute observer, acting in accord with the scientific standards of analysis. Art, philosophy, and literature would be shaped to resemble scientific thought. They would have to present clear, precise, and useful messages, all tied to an increased awareness of the nature of oppression and of the socialist revolution. "The philosophy of the Negro," proclaimed the *Messenger*, "will be a scientific philosophy and not some vague theological metaphysics."[35] "Negro art, music, and literature" would be brought under the umbrella of this approach. This culture would have immediate practical educational impact on its viewers:

> The sort of entertainment that is now being presented at the Lincoln Theatre cannot but carry tremendous social value. The pictures are the kind that lend aid and suggest and help one in adjusting one's self to society. They expose the pitfalls, the sores in our body social and bring to our minds a social doctrine that is clean, easy and simple.[36]

Such impact was only possible if the audience could recognize some aspect of its own existence on the stage:

> Take for instance, the character of Ibsen, above mentioned; I doubt if I know a Hedda Gabler, and probably there are but few average men who do. Therefore, the tragic in Hedda Gabler could not be as real and vivid to me as to another who may number such an individual among his or her female acquaintances. . . . It follows, all things being equal, the greatness of a tragedy depends upon its breadth of appeal![37]

"Naturalism" was, consequently, crucial. A "true" picture of human existence would have to be created. Just as the scientist seeks to discover and understand through observation, so too would the politically progressive artists present as clear a portrait as possible of the human condition. "Naturalism as expressed is hardly more than a photography of some phase of human existence without comment from the poet or author."[38]

The *Messenger* proposed to engage in both the liberation and the control of culture. Art and literature would be extracted from the capitalist cage, but they would immediately be made responsive to the demands of socialism. This position on liberated and controlled culture was grounded in the belief in the primacy of the economic issues. Culture would be freed from one form of economic system and put at the service of another. It is hardly surprising, in view of the *Messenger*'s stance on the primacy of economic forces and the subordination of culture, that they were highly critical of Du Bois.

The *Messenger* criticized Du Bois's *The Crisis* for befuddling readers with its claim that culture was central. The general confusion of black leaders, said the *Messenger*, "may be seen in Dr. Du Bois' *Crisis*":

> The leading column of the "Horizon" is always "Music and Art." Then "Meetings," which signify the gathering of literature. Next "The War," which inspires pictures and scenes for literary description and word painting. "Industry" and "Politics" sections follow. This is no coincidence, but a logical product of Du Bois' celebration. The *Messenger* carries as its first column, after editorials, "Economics and Politics." This is natural for us, because with us economics and politics take precedence to Music and Art."[39]

The problem with Du Bois and the other "Old Crowd," argued the *Messenger*, was that they were not scientific; they were trained in the humanities, in the classics. We need those trained in the science of society, the science of profound social change, not writers and artists, said the black socialists. "The hope of the race rests in new leaders with a more thorough grasp of scientific education and a calm but uncompromising courage."[40]

For the *Messenger*, Du Bois's fundamental error was his belief in the significance of culture. Said one *Messenger* writer, Du Bois mistakes the effect for the cause, as he does when he lays the ground for the new order on the basis of a moral system. It may be said, however, that ethical principles are merely the outgrowths of the social system. They are the products of the socio-economic order and never the cause of it.[41]

Du Bois in all his poetic passion had lost sight of the material foundations of society. Poems did not change the world; rather, the world was changed by real transformations in the system of production. All else followed from those transformations.

For the *Messenger*, those engaged in the making of art, literature, and philosophy could play useful roles in the struggle for freedom only through an economic reformulation of their work. It was only by changing the mode of their production through unions and other worker types of organization that the culture makers would be able to effectively join in the struggle. Concomitantly, their creative output would reflect that change in the mode of their production. Their work would have to become more scientific and practical. The artists, writers, and philosophers could not, in this view, form a group of their own, for their potential as activists lay not in their artistry but in their productiveness as culture workers. They could be useful only as part of a broader, disciplined, economically oriented movement.

In this discussion of the *Messenger*, we see a basic coherence in the stance taken in this magazine. First and foremost, economic forces were assigned the central role. The mode of production shaped global oppression. The socialist mode of production would end that oppression. All the subjugated workers were held together by their common chains. Other forms of identity were not significant except as they distracted attention from the real economic issues. A major problem, the *Messenger* editors felt, was the misleading claims of other leaders who suggested that noneconomic dimensions were important. For the *Messenger*, the position of Du Bois, which placed culture in the center, was a notorious example of such distraction from the real economic task of liberation. The masses, although infused with a vital energy, could not by themselves develop an understanding of the global economic nature of their struggle. Consequently, it was necessary that those who did recognize the importance of scientific analysis of economic forces, and who could use this analysis to channel the raw energy of the masses, take the high ground of black leadership. These "New Crowd Negroes" would marshall and shape black workers as part of the general proletarian battle against capitalism.

Within this framework of the scientific socialist black vanguard, the Du Boisan humanists could not be accepted as the leading group. They could play a supporting role, but only if they reorganized themselves according to the principles laid down by the socialists. They would have to transform their flights of artistic and literary imagination into rigorous scientific naturalism. They would have to organize themselves into collectives and unions. In this way they could join with the mass of workers and be led by the enlightened socialist cadres.

The *Messenger* had no more room for the masses at the pinnacle of leadership than it did for competing humanistic elites. For the *Messenger*, the urbanizing black masses, seen as part of the world-wide proletariat, were the wellspring from which revolutionary change would issue. Unlike the conservative "Old Crowd" black elites, whose cultured ways had sapped their vitality, the masses had a raw and splendid energy—the volcanic potential of the "uncultured"—from which great changes would flow.[42] The *Messenger's* sense of the black masses as part of the world-wide proletariat clearly reflected a movement away from the more agrarian and Southern oriented formulations of Washington and the early Du Bois. (We should note in passing that the *Messenger* generally ignored Du Bois's trenchant analysis of how the European labor elite was entangled in the rape of Africa and Asia.) But for all its faith in the power of the black proletariat, the *Messenger* saw the black masses as being in deep need of scientific, disciplined, socialist leadership, such as that offered by Chandler Owen and A. Philip Randolph.

This view ill-equipped the *Messenger* for grappling with the increasing urbanization and cosmopolitanism of black people. The *Messenger* basically ignored these developments in the black population. It saw global awareness, cosmopolitanism, only among the scientific socialists who grasped the enormous world-wide revolution that was taking place. Cosmopolitan understanding among everyday people was rejected as an impossibility.

The *Messenger* represented a major effort to take Booker T. Washington's materialist-economic type of Vanguard perspective from its post-Reconstruction, agrarian Southern context and place it in a post–war, modern, urbanizing, more cosmopolitan environment. The *Messenger*'s socialist editors shared with Washington the essential emphasis on the centrality of economic forces as the propellants of social change. They defined those forces differently. For Washington, capitalism was progressive. For the *Messenger*, capitalism would have to be overcome. Yet both approaches denied that culture could be viewed as the central arena of struggle. Both Washington and the *Messenger*, considered Du Bois's focus on culture as dangerously fallacious. Washington's dictum "The study of art that does not result in making the strong less willing to oppress the weak means little," [43] is not much different from one *Messenger* writer's statement that, "when the shooting starts," he would rather "be a crack shot than the most finished Homeric scholar in the land." [44] This common rejection of the emphasis on culture helps us to understand how the "conservative" Washington and the "radical" *Messenger* could both oppose Du Bois.

The New Negro

In 1925, at the heart of that flowering of arts and letters now known as the Harlem Renaissance, *The New Negro*, a collection of essays edited by Alain Locke, was published. Running through most of the book was a strong sense of a distinctive modern outlook developing among the urban black intellectuals, literati, and artists. Although Locke did not invent the term "New Negro," his book was infused with the important notion that a politically conscious cosmopolitan black elite was arising to lead their people from bondage.

As Robert Hayden says, Locke's book "had the effect of a manifesto."[45]

Just as the *Messenger* continued the tradition of the older Washingtonian materialist-economic type of Vanguard perspective in a modern urbane setting, so *The New Negro* took up the idealistic type of Vanguard perspective pioneered by Du Bois, focusing on culture and consciousness as the central arena of struggle. Like the *Messenger*, *The New Negro* assumed the need for elite vanguard leadership of what were viewed as the backward black masses.

The New Negro included a wide variety of essays, stories, poems, and illustrations. Contained in the work were important essays by James Weldon Johnson, the poet and novelist; Charles W. Johnson, research director for the National Urban League, who had studied under Robert Park; Melville Herskovits, the anthropologist and only non-black contributor to the volume; Jessie Fauset, literary editor of the NAACP journal, *The Crisis*; and of course, Alain Locke, Rhodes scholar, professor of literature at Howard University, and chief philosopher of the Harlem Renaissance.

One of the major themes in *The New Negro* was that black people were fully citizens of the United States. This emphasis was most directly developed in the article by Melville Herskovits, "The Negro's Americanism." For those who know him as a pioneer in the discovery of Africanisms in the New World, these earlier arguments by Herskovits may come as a surprise.[46] Herskovits asserted that black people of the United States had in no way maintained a distinctive African-rooted culture. For Herskovits, Harlem was excellent evidence for this position: "In Harlem, we have today, essentially a typical American community." Black people in general, argued Herskovits, "have absorbed the culture of America . . . they have absorbed it as all the great racial and social groups in this country have absorbed it." Moreover, he proclaimed, "Of the African culture, not a trace. Even the spirituals are an expression of the emotion of the Negro playing through the religious patterns of white America."[47] If Harlem and other black communities had any distinctive features (and Herskovits did not describe any here), these could be considered to be mere "remnants" from the "peasant days in the South." In sum, Harlem was "part of the larger whole of the city," and as such it represented, "as do all American communities which it resembles, a case of complete acculturation."[48]

Herskovits described this acculturated community in the following way:

> And so I went, and what I found was churches and schools, club houses and lodge meeting-places, the library and the newspaper offices and the Y.M.C.A. and the busy One Hundred Thirty-fifth Street and the hospitals and the social service agencies. I met persons who were lawyers and doctors and editors and writers, who were chauffeurs and peddlers and longshoremen and real estate brokers and capitalists, teachers and nurses and students and writers and cooks. And all Negroes' cabarets and theaters, drug stores and restaurants just like those everywhere else. And finally after a time, it occurred to me that what I was seeing was a community, just like any other American community. The same pattern only a different shade.[49]

This stance, that Harlem was a community like any other, must be viewed in the oppressive context of the time. We can easily see that this depiction of the Americanness of Harlem could be an important buttress against claims that blacks were inferior. Since some of the claims were based on the supposed differences between black and white people, any evidence of commonality across racial lines was a blow for progress. Herskovits, an anthropologist, added the weight of authority to his walking-tour observations. He contended that the worldview of black people was not essentially different from that of white Americans. "Wherever we might go, we find the Negro reacting to the same situations in much the same fashion as his white brother." If there was any difference between blacks and whites it might reflect not scientifically verifiable evidence but rather a "certain emotional quality," which could not be measured but must be "sensed." Aside from this vague suggestion about possible psychological differences, Herskovits asserted the Americanness of Harlem and its inhabitants.

Nor was Herskovits alone in taking this tack. James Weldon Johnson also saw black society as integrated into the wider American context. Harlem, said Johnson, was "the greatest Negro city in the world." It was, however, not at all similar to the ethnic "quarters," such as the "Little Italies" and "Chinatowns." Rather, Harlem was "more metropolitan and more a part of New York all the while."[50] There were important reasons for the metropolitan New York character of Harlem:

> First, the language of Harlem is not alien; it is not Italian or Yiddish, it is English. Harlem talks American, reads American, thinks American. Second, Harlem is not physically a "quarter." It is not a section cut off. It is merely a zone through which four main arteries of the city run. Third, the fact that there is little or no gang labor gives Harlem Negroes the opportunity for individual expansion and individual contacts with the life and spirit of New York.[51]

Johnson continued, "The rapidity with which Negroes become good New Yorkers is one of the marvels to observe." "The Negro," he said, "loves New York." Harlem would become "the intellectual, the cultural, and the financial center for Negroes of the United States."[52] But it would do so as an American community whose only major distinctive feature was that it consisted largely of black people. In all other respects, it was clearly a part of the wider society. Johnson certainly agreed with Herskovits that Harlem was like other American communities "only a different shade"!

Other essays in *The New Negro* proclaimed the social stability of Harlem. These arguments were a response to depictions of blacks as barbaric. The image of well-ordered community life was yet another weapon in the arsenal against racism. In this vein, J. W. Johnson noted that Harlem was

> not a slum or a fringe; it is located in the heart of Manhattan and occupies one of the most beautiful and healthful sections of the city. It is not a "quarter" of dilapidated tenements, but is made up of new-law apartments and handsome dwellings, with well-paved and well-lighted streets. . . . A stranger who rides up magnificent Seventh

Avenue on a bus or in an automobile must be struck with surprise at the transformation which takes place after he crosses One Hundred and Twenty-fifth Street. Beginning there, the population suddenly darkens and he rides through twenty-five solid blocks where the passers-by, the shoppers, those sitting in restaurants, coming out of theaters, standing in doorways and looking out of windows are practically all Negroes. . . .[53]

All these black people, said Johnson, were busily and effectively engaged in the life of a dynamic, expanding community. The result was the development of a healthy society: "Harlem is a Negro community, well defined and stable, anchored to its fixed homes, churches, institutions, businesses and amusement places; having its own working business, and professional classes."[54]

Johnson noted that there were certain "unique characteristics" on the surface of Harlem life such as "color, gaiety, singing, dancing, boisterous laughter and loud talk."[55] But this was a mere "coloring" that in no way disrupted the fundamental Americanness of life there. Johnson here attempted to take the very images that white Americans had used as "evidence" of black "primitiveness" and to show them as parts of civilized urban existence. Black people could be "boisterous" and full of "color" but they did so within a community that had all the features of other American communities.

The articles by J. W. Johnson and Herskovits emphasized the stable American nature of Harlem, the "Negro capital," and by implication all other black communities as well. Other writers in *The New Negro* focused on the great cultural breakdown that the movement north entailed for the black masses. Charles Johnson saw this breakdown as a matter of cultural transformation. "In ten years," he noted, "Negroes have been actually transplanted from one culture to another." The nature of this transplantation to an urban setting Johnson continued, involved a significant loss of rural forms of organization and thought. In the rural towns, said Johnson, "Church, lodge, gossip, respect of friends, established customs, social and racial, exercise controls."

But such forms of control and established customs could not hold in the city:

> Where once there were personal and intimate relations, in which individuals were in contact at practically all points of their lives, there are now group relations in which the whole structure is broken up and reassorted, casting them in contact at only one or two points of their lives. The old controls are no longer expected to operate. Whether apparent or not, the newcomers are forced to reorganize their lives, to enter new status and adjust to it that eager restlessness which prompted them to leave home. In the new environment there are many and varied substitutes which answer more or less directly the myriad desires indiscriminately comprehended by the church. . . . When the old ties are broken new satisfactions are sought.[56]

Sometimes these new satisfactions were positive and uplifting. The Y.M.C.A., for example, offered one form of social sustenance in the teeming city. Yet there was also a loss of family control resulting from the breakdown between rural parents and their rapidly urbanizing and assimilating children. "But too often, as with European immigrants, the family loses control over the children who become assimilated more rapidly than their parents. Tragic evidence of this appear coldly detailed in the records of delinquency."[57] Consequently, the move from rural to urban was turbulent and crisis ridden. Both the comforting intimacy and constraining, narrow oppressiveness of the rural south were left behind. In their place new organizations and beliefs were encountered, some helpful, some dangerous.[58] But the real difficulty, argued Johnson, lay not in the increase in forms of social distress such as juvenile delinquency among the new migrants to the city. The more profound problem was to be found in the lag between the change taking place as people became city residents and their comprehension of that change. The black masses in the city did not fully understand the situation that confronted them. In the "recognization of their attitudes," said Johnson, there "is racial as well as social disorientation."[59] The culture of rural black America was being radically altered by urbanization in ways mysterious to the people themselves. As yet, they could only dimly perceive the forces that were casting them into a new mold.

Arthur Huff Fauset took the Charles Johnson position even further. Fauset definitively declared that there had been indeed a distinctive Afro-American rural culture. This culture was an outgrowth of the whole people, the "folk." Unlike Herskovits, Fauset saw this rural folk culture as having deep ties to the more ancient African past. There was no doubt as to "the antiquity and authentic folk-lore ancestry" of Afro-American rural culture.[60] Fauset argued that the original producers of the folk culture were vanishing under the impact of urbanization. In the process of becoming "modern" and "urban," black people were turning away from a rich body of literature and lore that they themselves had created. "Some of the precious secrets of folk history," he wrote, "are in danger of fading out in its gradual disappearance."[61] In the process, both the creative energies of the rural Southern black people and the "distinctively African" elements of their culture were vanishing.

Alain Locke agreed, and extended the argument. The move to the city involved both a breakdown of old ways *and* the potential for the creation of new positive ways of life. Life in the city, he argued, was bound to involve "renewed self-respect and self-dependence, the life of the Negro community is bound to enter a new dynamic phase. . . ."[62] The impetus for such a phase, however, could not be expected to develop from the grass roots because the black masses were, in Locke's view, still too disorganized to act. Along with Johnson and Fauset, he saw the problems inherent in a situation in which a loss of culture occurred simultaneously with the failure of a people to develop a new consciousness to fit their new urban surroundings.

The emphasis of Locke, Fauset, and Charles Johnson on the disintegrating effects of the city simultaneously focused attention on the cultural creations of black people and emphasized the fundamental weakness of those creations. Black people had indeed created their own particular culture. Fauset even maintained that it had an African dimension.

But this creation had been accomplished without understanding and deliberation. The people's culture was a natural effort, more raw than articulate. "No sane observer," proclaimed Locke, "would contend that the great masses are articulate as yet."[63] The strength of the people was to be found in precisely their unconscious "emotional intuition."[64] Locke said that theirs was "the instinctive gift of the folk-spirit."[65]

Terms that emphasize the "natural," "instinctual," inarticulate "spirit" of the folk pervade *The New Negro*. The people have energy, but they are unconscious, unaware, somnambulistic. Theirs was the "slumbering gift of folk temperament."[66] But because the folk were now flocking to the cities and casting their gift aside, culture itself would be changed by the onslaught of industrialization and urbanization. A crucial juncture had been reached. Fragile folk culture faced the overwhelming might of modern industrial society. The intuitive creations of the folk were in danger of being lost forever.

In *The New Negro*, the primacy of consciousness and the central role of the intellectuals became the main emphasis. The complexities of the transformation from the plantation-rural to the modern-urban could only be comprehended by an elite group. The confused black masses would need "a new leadership," and "a new orientation."[67] The black leaders would close the gap between the urban reality and the undeveloped consciousness of recent immigrants from the South. Such leaders would have to consciously build on the remains of folk culture, of which only they were aware, in order to create a new culture that would be meaningful and useful to the black masses in the cities. The main task, the primary struggle, would be to develop new ways of thinking. The sense of black inferiority would have to be replaced by a sense of equality.

Charles Johnson concurred that the answer to the problem of culture loss was to be found in a culturally conscious black vanguard. This "new" black leadership, housed in the cities but cognizant of the importance of "folklore," was beginning to integrate the new urban conditions with the cultural past. In so doing, this leadership would help prevent a complete capitulation to the domination of the wider society and help develop an urban black culture. "The newer voices," wrote Johnson, "at a more comfortable distance, are beginning to find a new beauty in these heritages, and new values in their own lives."[68] Locke agreed with Johnson that black intellectuals had to take control in fashioning a new black culture. The sense was that the past, properly directed and transformed by the "newer voices," could assist in the creation of the essential "new values" necessary for success in industrial America. The task of developing these values was to be taken on by the "New Negro,"—a vanguard group of black intellectuals.

The New Negro did not portray this vanguard group as a social isolate. They were viewed as a product of an urban environment, which in its turn was a result of the mass migration of black people out of the rural South. Without this fundamental social fact, said Locke, the intellectuals would not exist. The vital, raw energy of the people powered the black vanguard elite. "In a real sense," wrote Locke, "it is the rank and file who are leading, and the leaders who are following."[69] Yet, as we probe this sense of the "leadership of the rank and file," we see that the people were leading only through their raw, inarticulate energy. Further, the people's leadership, left to itself, would tend, in Johnson's argument, toward disastrous ends. The intellectuals needed the energy of the people, but the people needed the intellectuals for fundamental guidance.

The "guidance" that the New Negro would offer, said Locke, involved a conscious transformation of the vital, yet unformed, energy of the masses. Crucial to Locke's arguments was the assertion that the black elite was conscious rather than primordially naturalistic. The New Negro, he wrote, "now becomes a conscious contributor and lays aside the status of beneficiary and ward." The result would be "the releasing of our talented group from the arid fields of controversy and debate to the productive fields of creative expression." Only through an analytically reflective transformation of the cultural past could the domination by the wider society be blunted. The problem with "unconscious" black folk-culture, said Locke, was that much of it had been "absorbed" by the white South.[70] "Folk art," argued Locke, was a "fragile vehicle" left to its own devices.[71] Simultaneously, this fragile art of the folk had a certain power of "emotional intuition," a certain raw energy.[72] Thus, folk art was at once fragile and strong. It was strong as a basic human response to the dilemmas of life, yet weak because its intuitive understanding failed to comprehend its own deeper meanings.

For Locke, then, a central task for the intellectuals was to transform folk art into modern forms of art, to create a genuine culture from the fragments of folk culture. Needed was a vital "modern interpretation" that would, for example, relate folk songs "to the folk activities that they motivated, classifying them by their respective song-types."[73] The emphasis on classification was typical of Locke. The intuitive creations of the folk were to be classified as an initial step toward transforming them into a different form of art. It is important, said Locke, that the "Negro is being carefully studied."[74] Through such analysis, the culture of the folk would be transformed into a more sophisticated and self-conscious form. The role of the intellectual was clear: "Maintaining spiritual kinship with the best traditions of this great folk art he must make himself the recognized vehicle of both its transmission and its further development."[75] It would be through the rigorous, sophisticated, and scientific methods of the black intellectuals that folk art would become fine art and that a dying culture would be brought to new life.

Accordingly, Fauset argued for the importance of "scientific" investigations of folk-lore:

> The antiquity and authentic folk-lore ancestry of the Negro talk make it the proper study for the scientific folklorist rather than the literary amateur. It is the ethnologist, the philologist, and the student of primitive psychology that are most needed for its present investigation.[76]

When carried out by black scholars, this scientific work would not be simply a detached form of analysis and observation. Because of the scholars' commonality with the folk culture under investigation, the "spirit" of the folk would be faithfully followed. Abandoned by the urbanizing black masses, folk culture was not only to be salvaged but reformed into a new urban culture by the black vanguard. Without such analytical formulation, much of the past would lie fallow. Most black people, Locke argued, approached Africa with "as alienated and misunderstanding an attitude as the average European Westerner."[77] An informed black intelligentsia would be able to employ elements of the past and to synthesize a cultural foundation upon which the "as yet inarticulate masses" could build.

As Henry Louis Gates has pointed out, the very concept of the "New Negro" proclaims a break with the past, a severe differentiation of these Negroes from the other ones.[78] Locke did not invent the term "New Negro" nor was he the first to propose the existence of a black vanguard or "talented tenth." What is distinctively important about his proposal is the claim that the elite leadership will know more about the people's culture than its very creators. Locke's conception of the Vanguard thus had a very particular tone. His was an elite that claimed a firm grounding in the culture of the people, but it was a grounding attained only by sophisticated cultural analysis. In the mass, the people were not able to comprehend, use, or defend their own productions. The new black intellectuals would do what the masses of people could not: they would transform folk art into fine art. The elite therefore, were essential to the survival of black culture and progress.

Indeed, the elite assumed that among the masses, folk culture was lost or dying. The rural roots of the culture were disappearing. The culture had become essentially artifactual. It was the elite who could transform the artifacts into living forms that could be the basis for "new" black society. Thus, precisely at the moment that *The New Negro* writers were proclaiming their commonality with the people, they were declaring their tremendous differences from them. The people were misdirected and "inarticulate as yet." It was the artifacts of their forebears, now unencumbered by living use, that the intellectuals would reshape for their purposes.

The *New Negro* rejection of the "old Negro" actually represented an overt break with the present, a rejection of the people as they were. Johnson's warning that the people were rejecting their culture was essentially a condemnation of the people. Through "rigorous analysis" of selective elements of folklore, the self-asserted vanguard group would reclaim positive elements from the past and at the same time disassociate themselves from the untutored masses.

In adopting the idealistic approach of Du Bois, *The New Negro* distinguished itself from the *Messenger's* continuation of Washington's materialistic focus. Neither the *Messenger* or *The New Negro* made much effort to accommodate their Vanguard perspectives to the changing circumstances of an ever more urbanized and cosmopolitan black population. To the contrary, they both attempted to mold urban circumstances into older conceptual frameworks based on agrarian post-Reconstruction environments. The Vanguard's bleak turn-of-the-century picture of mass disorganization among black people was simply laid over the increasingly urbane cosmopolitan environment of the era following the First World War. The great degree of globalization, the real increase in interconnectedness and awareness among major portions of the black population, were not acknowledged. Instead, globalization and cosmopolitanism were seen as being restricted to the so-called "thinking elements" of the black population—the intellectuals, the literati, the artists, and the socialists. The capacity of everyday people to creatively and consciously generate social order was not recognized.

4

Non-Elite Social Action

George W. Ellis, Arturo Schomburg,
and the Universal Negro
Improvement Association

While the proponents of the Vanguard perspective ignored the increasingly cosmopolitan nature of the black
population, others were more open to the possibilities of
creative resistance among the people at large. Taking a Mutualistic approach, they looked at the way in which various
people in many walks of life had created social organizations
resistent to oppression and offering a framework of positive
change. Two writers who exemplified this approach were
George W. Ellis, a black lawyer and ethnographer, and
Arturo (Arthur) Schomburg, a bibliophile of Africana literature whose views on popular culture were vital to the Mutualistic viewpoint. Ellis and Schomburg paved the way for
the Universal Negro Improvement Association, best known
for its magnetic and controversial leader Marcus Garvey.

Ellis and Schomburg are a pair of black writers who emphasized a multi-dimensional struggle for freedom. Schomburg chose to emphasize continuities. For him there were no
major breaks between the African past, the time of slavery,
and the black presence in the industrial urban North. Each
of these were different historic moments but one led to the

other. The pathway that linked these moments was constructed by people. In Schomburg's view, the people carried with them elements from the past, even as they reconstituted and transformed these elements into the present.

The people were conscious creators of complex bodies of knowledge. As such they were fundamentally no different from the specialist groups of black scholars whose skills were directed at particular kinds of knowledge. Consequently there could be no major division between the people and their intellectuals. Furthermore, in the long run the creations of the intellectuals, in particular their recapturing of black history, would merge with the people's knowledge to form a whole. The way to this merger was smoothed, in Schomburg's view, because all science was ideologically driven and informed. Sometimes this connection was dangerous, as when science was controlled by racism. At other times it could be progressive, as when engaged black scholars employed their scholarship to forge racial unity.

Similarly, Ellis considered that science had been ideologically shaped to the detriment of black people, but it could be made to serve the process of black liberation. Scholars could therefore play an important role in the black struggle. Yet this role could not be central. With Schomburg, Ellis emphasized that the people in general, through their political actions, would develop a group consciousness even as engaged black scholars were adding their own contribution to that development.

An Ethnographer of Social Action

George W. Ellis is a forgotten figure, whose important work is largely unknown. W. E. B. Du Bois praised Ellis's major 1915 ethnographic work, *Negro Culture in West Africa*.[1] St. Clair Drake, the dean of Afro-American anthropology, described Ellis as a pioneer in anthropology.[2] Rayford Logan and Michael Winston see Ellis as a "much neglected figure who deserves full biographic treatment."[3] Aside from such observations, there is little commentary on Ellis.

Trained as a lawyer, active in Republican and Progressive Party politics in Illinois in the early 1900s, George Washington Ellis also spent eight years as secretary to the American legation to Liberia. Upon his return to the United States in 1910, he became assistant corporation counsel to the city of Chicago.[4] In Africa, where he engaged in important ethnographic work among the Vai peoples, and in the United States, Ellis strove to understand how "the darker races" could progress from oppression to freedom. As he analyzed various examples of change in both Africa and Afro-American society, Ellis developed, albeit in a fragmentary way, an approach that was decidedly different from that of the Vanguard perspective.

Like the Vanguard perspective writers, Ellis was concerned with the strategies by which black people could advance themselves. Yet for Ellis, the most successful approaches would be those that allowed for the introduction of diverse skills from many sources. Where the Vanguard would identify a domain of central social importance and a leading group to further it, Ellis took a more multidimensional view of the world. Ellis transformed the term "culture." For him, culture included not just the arts and literature but technology, economic activity, and political activity as well. Culture, then, could only be the creation of many people, not of one group. Ellis's major ethnographic work was entitled *Negro Culture in West Africa*, by which he meant everything from farming to sculpture.

Upon Ellis's return from legation duty in Liberia in 1910, he increasingly wrote articles on Afro-American politics, culture, and society. His wide range of interests is not surprising for in his analysis of Afro-America, Ellis worked out the ideas of social action as involving both transformation and persistence of black society in the United States. In his writings on Afro-America, he emphasized the importance of multiple approaches to progress, given that the oppression facing black people was itself multidimensional. Change, for Ellis, could not come from one quarter or through one particular group; it would have to involve struggle in a number of areas by people from diverse walks of life.

To understand Ellis's thoughts on political struggle, let

us begin by looking at his writings on the role of scholarship. Ellis argued that, rather than carrying out a detached search for truth, scholars were instruments of their political systems. Claims of objectivity only made their work sharper as an ideological weapon. The ideological nature of many scholars' work was clear, argued Ellis, in regard to the issue of race. Certain ethnologists had played a major role in buttressing claims of white superiority through their academic work:

> Toward making permanent the prejudice between the white and colored races, ethnologist have played an important part, by placing upon ill-founded and erroneous conclusions concerning the white and colored races the stamp and authority of science. . . . Ethnological writers like Gobineau of France and Ammon of Germany taught and established the false theories that the races were naturally unequal.[5]

Such ethnological evils were not, however, the major source of the oppressive inflammation that infected science. The main example of the relationship between scholarship and racism was to be found in the "doctrine of evolution" that had spread throughout society:

> Concomitant with this anti-Negro ethnological propaganda, Darwin, Wallace, Huxley, Spencer, Haeckal, and others, announced the doctrine of evolution and supported it with such force by evidences from all the allied and other sciences, that the leaders of modern philosophy, religion and science, accepted this principle and ultimately embraced [it]. . . . In the light of this view, more than other races, the proximity of the Negro to the anthropoid apes—the gorilla, gibbon, chimpanzee, and the orang-utang—was believed to have additional scientific proof and demonstration.[6]

This fusion of ethnology and biology had a devastating political effect on the relations between the black and white peoples, Ellis argued. The learned opinions of ethnologists and biologists did not stay contained in academia; they spread like wildfire across an already volatile landscape and found a ready reception among those already convinced of the superiority of the whites:

> For several generations from the fortified ramparts of school, college, university, literature, and science, the white mind was so assiduously assailed and so constantly besieged, that the white race was thoroughly inoculated and filled with the viruses and poison of race prejudice. It is through these potent agencies and powerful channels that the ethnological science has been such an influential factor in creating, diffusing and crystallizing race prejudice in the social mind of the whites, by the use of false data and ill-founded opinions against the Negro, in the educational and social system.[7]

From the highest levels of academia, the systematic falsities of white superiority were transformed into a popular message by newspapers that took already extravagant lies and ground them down into popular simplicities:

> The great newspapers of the country have cooperated in the propaganda of race prejudice by making the crime of every Negro racial rather than individual, and employing the use of the word, "Negro" in glaring head-lines for no other purpose than to inflame the popular mind against this race, and to teach the false doctrine that the Negro is more criminally and naturally inferior to other race groups.[8]

Such false doctrines contributed, said Ellis, to "riot and mob rule."[9] Ellis traced the path extending from textbook to lynch rope. He did not stop at this level of ideological analysis. Certainly, the manipulation of the public mind by a press fed by "science" was a potent reality. Research, however, did not exist in isolation. Scholars did not create racist theories in a vacuum. Rather, from Ellis's perspective, they were performing a certain function, however much they might protest their servile role.

The beginnings of racist scholarship were to be found, Ellis asserted, in the institution of slavery. Because it was ethically indefensible, slavery required a body of discourse to justify its existence. A cluster of tame house scholars was required to "prove" the inferiority of the black race. Quite clearly, said Ellis, "false racial philosophies were put forth to conserve the vested slave interest of the world." [10] With the abolition of slavery, the ideological function of racist science did not end, but its method was altered: "The scholars of the master class who employed their scholarship to justify the enslavement of the Negro lost their cause and they are now succeeded by a school which seeks to justify the subservience of the Negro race." [11]

Ellis was not timid in proclaiming the solution to this ideological scholarship. A direct, devastating, and complete attack had to be launched against it. The real problem, said Ellis, was to make the truth public and "to expunge from the literature of this and other countries the false doctrines and statements therein concerning the races of men." [12] There was, Ellis suggested, another sort of scholarship that promised to cut away much of the propaganda that had been scientifically enshrined. Ethnologist s such as Franz Boas and Thomas Chamberlain, both of whom wrote extensively for the *Journal of Race Development* to which Ellis contributed, were making a "new ethnology," [13] which challenged the very foundations of the older racist theorists. Through the work of Boas and others, said Ellis:

> We have not only learned the error of the scientific and literary advocates of the Caucasian slave-vested interests in this country and abroad and their present representatives who plead for Negro race subservience, but we have learned much truth concerning what are called the Caucasian and Negro races. [14]

Such work demonstrated the falsity of white claims of racial superiority. The principal theoretical development was, for Ellis, the discovery that all peoples were of one species and that the "races" were but variations, and minor ones at that. There could be no claims of basic biological superiority of one race over another. Furthermore, historically the new scholarship also demonstrated the diverse origins of civilization among non-white peoples. Whites, then, could claim neither biological nor historical support for their vaunted superiority.

Ellis argued that scholarly activity had to be moved from the ideological position of racism to the ideological position of democracy. Without such a movement, the intellectuals would continue to be the "scholars of the masterclass" whose work would assist in the oppression of the peoples of color rather than in their attainment of true and practical freedom.[15]

Given the multiplicity of his concerns, it is hardly surprising that Ellis should suggest that scholars and writers were not at the center of social change. A new democratically infused scholarship was needed, but it would hardly be enough in itself. Ellis was also concerned that everyday black Americans develop an analytical awareness of oppression and of the means of resistance. Such consciousness would be furthered through people's direct political actions. But Ellis was certain that this awareness would be developed in part through formal education. Here, too, he shared some of Dewey's views on the importance of education in the strengthening of democratic community.

Because Ellis held formal education to be one of the major avenues by which peoples' critical consciousness was developed, he was concerned with the state of schooling available to black Americans. Unlike Booker T. Washington who saw the miseducation of black people in the South as an irrational outcome of racism, Ellis considered it part and parcel of the control of that population. He declared that, "in the South efforts were made to discourage the North in giving funds for the education of black children. . . . The facilities of schools for Negro children are inferior to those for whites and the terms are often shorter outside of the large cities." Such institutional deficiencies were deliberately aimed at keeping black people in a position of subordination: "It is the purpose to give the Negro just such education as will enable the race to best serve the whites and as will keep the Negro satisfied in his new status of freedom."[16]

The schooling of black youth, said Ellis, was not just poor and lacking in quality. On the contrary, that schooling was very well designed; its aim was to keep black people in positions of semi-serfdom. By restricting instruction to the most limited manual skills, the white South would prevent the practical progress of black students. And such schooling would reduce not just the level of skills but the level of consciousness as well. Ellis emphasized that "such education" would keep "the Negro satisfied" in "his subordinate position." The dominant idea of Southern education for the black person "is such as will best fit him to obey and serve the white race, with all its inherited and acquired psychic antipathy and sociological prejudice against the darker races."[17]

The economic trends in the South support Ellis's contention that inferior education for black children aided in the capitalist development of that region, rather than Washington's notion that racism was an aberration detrimental to business. The industrialization of the South that began in the 1880s characteristically employed blacks only at the most unskilled, low-paying jobs. Black workers thus were concentrated in agriculture and domestic and personal services that did not require a better-educated black labor force. Thus, as Ellis saw, education played a role in the sustaining economic subjugation of the black population.

It is useful to note, with Harold Barron, that exclusion of black workers "from industry was not based on rational calculation regarding the characteristics of the labor supply." To the contrary, Southern employers often indicated that "medium skilled" black workers were a "remarkable success." In a 1901 survey, over 60 percent of the employers regarded their black workers "as good or better than their white workers."[18] In fact, Southern business could have made use of a better-educated black work force. The issue, however, was stability. Better educated black workers who competed with their white counterparts could be a source of friction in an already volatile situation. The "Northern ruling class," as Barron points out, was concerned with conditions that "stabilized the national political system," and "they supported the establishment of a subservient black peasantry" in the late 1880s and early 1900s.[19] Here is where Ellis's sense of the role played by education is accurate. Washington's view would have been pertinent had capitalist need for labor become more intense and required some change in the relations of business with blacks.

Without an emphasis on "education for truth, virtue, development, freedom and service," educated blacks were subject to continual servility, Ellis argued.[20] Such subordination was complex, being enforced and reinforced by a multitude of methods, some overtly coercive and others more indirect. Limited education was an indirect, but important, method of control. Consequently, Ellis advocated a liberated educational system. He declared that the development of democracy was only possible when there was a well-educated and consciously alert population. For the South to use education as a means of controlling the black population amounted to the prevention of democracy.

But despite the importance of institutionalized education, human progress also required conscious direct action. One major form of direct action was the revolutionary moment. The French and Haitian Revolutions were two such examples. Ellis wrote that the impact of these two revolutions traveled beyond their particular circumstances:

> The French Revolution destroyed Bourbon rule in France in the death and execution of Louis XVI, yet the mighty tumult of this popular outbreak for the rights of man shook every throne in Europe and gave to democracy a footing and a hearing around the world. . . .

Similarly, in Haiti

> the first great stroke which announced the ultimate decay and death of Negro slavery and the extension of democracy to include the Negro races was made when Toussaint L'Overture in the closing years of the eighteenth century rose up in Haiti and successfully led the blacks in revolution against their oppressors. Democracy, therefore was secured for the blacks in very much the same manner as it was secured for the whites.[21]

The steps toward democracy did not always have to be so cataclysmic. There is a sense in Ellis of both an evolutionary and a revolutionary development. Each major step could itself be revolutionary, sometimes in actuality and sometimes in a more covert way; but these were steps, nonetheless, in the growth of democracy. Through direct action, black people would learn to analyze and influence the political system. Such active participation, argued Ellis, was vital both to the successful participation of black people in the body politic and to the development of the black community as a power bloc. It was wrong, Ellis added, to think of development of distinctive black communities as simply and negatively a result of racism. More important was the positive group identification that sprang from coordinated political action:

> It is not to be understood that outside pressure or prejudice upon the Negro over the country and in Illinois of the past ten years is entirely responsible for the increased solidarity and extra political activity of the Negro in Chicago, for much of it is due to the gradual and evolutionary consciousness founded upon vast experiences in political recognition on the one hand, and the increased opportunity afforded by the primaries for independence and disinterested leadership on the part of the people with all the antecedent educational features of the other.[22]

The transformation of black communities into centers of influence, in Ellis's view, would require both practical political action and education. The people would be more disposed to educational programs illuminating the basis for group solidarity when they had actually engaged in acts of solidarity. Simultaneously, acts of solidarity would be enhanced by an analysis that exposed the corruption of city machine politics. A blend of critical analysis and practical action was needed, for one would not work without the other.

The success of truly democratic politics would amplify rather than diminish the distinctive identity of the black population. It would be as black communities that they would achieve political power and freedom. The black communities, shaped both by outside pressure and positive internal development, said Ellis, "have combined to solidify and to awaken the Negro in Chicago to a sense of his own power for self-defense and protection in an amazing and astonishing degree.[23] (Although it has taken many years, Ellis's understanding of the potential of the black vote in Chicago has been partially borne out in the early 1980s with the election of a black mayor and the decline of the machine politics that had kept black people out of that office.)

In addition to shaping their own communities by political activities, black people were also linking themselves to a world-circling movement of peoples of color to free themselves from white domination. From Africa to Japan, Ellis argued, a tremendous groundswell of resistance was developing. Black Americans were being lifted by that groundswell and consciously making themselves part of a worldwide movement. Ellis wrote:

> The birth and expansion of the Senussi movement in the African black belt, the dissemination of the propaganda of "Africa for Africans" in South Africa, the efforts for independence in India and Egypt, and the rapid assimilation of Western methods and culture by Japan and her sudden entrance into the first rank of the white nations, announced the gradual awakening of the colored races and the ultimate arrest and overthrow of the world sway and extension of white political supremacy over the colored peoples.[24]

In taking this tack, Ellis avoided the common American fallacy of viewing the black population as an isolate. Ellis saw American racial oppression as distinctive, yet part of a wider pattern. He also saw the resistance to that oppression in the United States as a distinctive part of a worldwide "awakening of the colored races." Black people, even in the smallest, most remote communities in the United States, were not acting alone; theirs was part of a global fight.

But although external oppression and internal political action were important for awakening the black population to its own power for "self-defense and protection," Ellis pointed to other factors that affected group consciousness. The black poet Paul Lawrence Dunbar wrote often in folk language or the "dialect" of the black South, arousing a storm of conflicting opinions among black intellectuals.[25] Some condemned it for being a racist depiction. Others praised it as echoing the very soul of the black race. Ellis observed that Dunbar's use of folk language was a partial product of racial exclusion: "This preference for Negro dialect poetry grew out of the intellectual and social prejudice of our country which indicated that if a Negro must be a poet he should confine himself to the Negro dialect alone."[26] Nonetheless, Ellis continued, Dunbar's creations were not simply a reaction to racial exclusion. Instead, Dunbar had transformed a negative situation into energetic poetic imagery. In part, this transformation of the racist pressure into the poetic imagination took the form of a universal transcendence. Ellis emphasized the universality of true poetry as a form of spiritual escape from the bounds of earthly transgressions and woes:

> The true province and function of poetry, therefore, is to give expression and voice, as far as possible, to the changes and transitions of emotion in the varying moods and passions of the soul and to inspire humanity toward that lofty goal described by Bacon:
>
> > Where the mind of man rests in Providence and turns upon the poles of truth.

Such poets "catch those deeper currents of life and nature."[27]

The value of Dunbar was not just in his transcendent universal qualities but also in the permutation that he performed on the racist structures that dictated his choice of dialect poetry. Even though that poetry had grown out of the "intellectual and social prejudice" of American society, Ellis felt that Dunbar's dialect poems "fairly teem with a natural inner wealth of Negro life and thought in almost every phase and feature. . . . He did, perhaps, what no poet of any other race would likely do, combined and preserved in poetic forms, the true and best life of the Negro race."[28] Ellis argued that, although Dunbar may have been forced by historic circumstances to write in "dialect," he recognized and celebrated the dignity and value of folk language in his use of it. This celebration was extremely important because the great evil of racist stereotypes was not simply that whites believed them, but that many black people accepted them as well. Dunbar, by refusing to be ashamed of dialect poetry, subverted the racist constraints that impelled him to write in such a style.[29] Dunbar's action was an important political statement that, while seeming to acquiesce to racist commands, was in fact a proclamation of the value of the culture created by black people in the South.

So, to the dimensions of education and political action, Ellis added the significance of literature that celebrated the strength and wisdom of the people. According to Ellis, Dunbar marched head on into the racist perceptions and emerged in control, owing to his pride in the dignity of black people as they actually were.

Ellis's description of Dunbar could just as easily refer to himself:

> In education, industry, science, art and literature Dunbar saw his race scaling the rugged heights of social progress in the long march toward true democracy. He felt all the pangs of their sorrow and suffering as their enemies were trying to starve and torture them back. With Miller, Du Bois, and Washington in command, the American division though under difficulties, is struggling upward and onward against the entrenched and fortified ramparts of race prejudice, race hatred, and race injustice, on toward the sun-crowned summits of liberty, equality and fraternity among all the races of men.[30]

Note in this passage the tone of the "long march" undertaken by a military-like "division" attacking the "ramparts of prejudice." Although Ellis was far from being a gradualist, he recognized that the struggle would be long; the enemy was well entrenched. If the marchers were energetic and determined, however, they could force the issue and create new circumstances. The struggle would have many dimensions, ranging from education and scholarship through art and literature to political action. No one domain was central, no one type of activity the most vital. Ellis's view of progress incorporates notions of evolutionary development with the quite different sense of people creating their own culture and politics. For Ellis, it was inconceivable that any part of the human race would be unable to develop in a progressive way. Black people could not be excluded from the general progressive tendency of humankind. Yet progress was not an automatic process but had to be created consciously.

Ellis saw the world moving toward democracy through long-term development. The "long march" of progress would be accomplished, in part, through vigorous practical leaps of direct action. The French and Haitian Revolutions were examples. But the American Revolution, with its proclamations of universal liberty and its actual support of slavery, testified to the limitations of even revolutionary moments. Nonetheless, it was significant, wrote Ellis, that the process of progress did have such moments, that it was not a sluggish, imperceptible drift upward.

The progression toward democracy proposed by Ellis involved a constant interplay of consciousness and direct action with the full possibility of cataclysmic moments of intense social change. Without the support of major changes in consciousness, Ellis considered that direct action would not be possible. Similarly, major changes in consciousness involved real action. Thus, Ellis sees a deep interrelationship between concrete tangible activity such as politics, and education, literature, and scholarship. He himself did not develop in any detail his image of mutual interplay among various people in different domains of social reality, but we can see that for him there is no one central societal dimension. Scholarship is important, but so is street-level politics. The work of the poets can stand alongside the local efforts of people to organize themselves. No one group is seen as having a monopoly on useful activity. Ellis sees all knowledge as partial, and so the group that seeks to bring its particular knowledge to bear cannot simply ride roughshod over all others but rather must look for ways to integrate its approach into existing forms. Ellis would probably have agreed with the character in Turgenev's novel *Smoke* who asked, "How can we borrow without consideration of the conditions of climate and of soil, the local and national peculiarities?"[31]

Intimately linked to Ellis's sense of the partiality of knowledge is his belief in the multifariousness of social reality. No person or group can cover all knowledge with a single message. Racial oppression in the United States was multifaceted. It reached into all parts of life, from the etiquette of personal relations to the structure of economic relations.

How then could there be one response that emphasized the social, or the economic, or the cultural, at the expense of the others? Resistance had to be as diverse and flexible as oppression. Ellis was certainly no anti-intellectual. He did not grovel before a plaster image of the "common man." But neither did he emphasize elite leadership. Ellis recognized no one center stage. For him, there were many stages and many actors, with scripts that were being constantly rewritten by the actors themselves.

A Chronicler of Popular Culture

Of African descent, Arturo (Arthur) Schomburg was born in San Juan, Puerto Rico. Educated in both public and private schools, he arrived in the United States in 1891, where he lived until his death in 1938. During those years he was a tireless and prolific collector of materials of the subject of black peoples in the New World. But he did more than collect. Schomburg strove to amass and analyze the material needed to construct an accurate black history. Standing at the institutional heart of culture in Harlem, he was a colleague of Alain Locke, president of the American Negro Academy; and co-founder of the Negro Society for Historical Research. He played an active role in the Negro Actors Guild, the Yoruba Literary and Debating Society, the Harriet Tubman Publishing Company, and various Ethiopian support groups during the Italo-Ethiopian War. His massive collection of materials on Afro-American life became the basis for the New York Public Library's Schomburg Center for Research in Black Culture.

Although generally described as bibliophile, a title which he certainly deserved, Schomburg also was an all-embracing cultural-historical investigator who laid the basis for a serious analysis of Afro-American life. His findings are scattered through a variety of articles in many kinds of publications.

Schomburg asserted that scientific investigation was intrinsically political, both in its origins and its content. With certain notable exceptions, Schomburg pointed out, Euro-American scholars denied any evidence that black people shared a common humanity with the rest of the world. At best, wrote Schomburg, accurate information was "widely dispersed and difficult to find."[32] At worst, the material available contained fraudulent and virulently racist sentiments. Schomburg complained, "The white historian to whom we are indebted for little that is right and much that is wrong has consistently and persistently proclaimed that in Africa is not a vestige of anything to show the handiwork of its black people."[33] His attack on this incomplete and distorted picture led him to compile list after list of black achievements that flew in the face of assertions of racial inferiority. From the ruins of Zimbabwe to the great university of Timbuktu, and from Pushkin and Dumas to Juan Latino, Schomburg hunted down evidence to contradict the prevailing contentions of Caucasian superiority.[34] The citing of these great peoples and places was not unique to Schomburg. Other writers such as William Ferris in *Africans Abroad* and Benjamin Brawley in *A Social History of the American Negro* had worked on such critical compilations.[35]

Schomburg was a diligent and intelligent gatherer of facts, his interests ranging from Spain to New Orleans and from Africa to Europe. He also attempted to develop a relativistic attitude to culture and knowledge in which the methods and beliefs of peoples of color would be seen, not just as objects of study, but as significant perspectives for understanding the world. His concern was not confined to scholarship but looked toward the creation of a cultural framework that would further the development and liberation of the "black race."

Schomburg's view of Africa, since he apparently never traveled there, is somewhat sketchy and derivative. Nonetheless, his work strains to present counterweight to the superior pretensions of European-American society. For example, Schomburg argued that the apparently inegalitarian societies of Africa headed by *obas* or kings had succeeded in providing security and sustenance for their citizens in a way that Western democracy, despite its claims, had not. The African mode of politics, said Schomburg, had overcome the problem of the "large number of paupers and beggers" that revealed the fundamental weakness of "our modern civilization":

> for in fact wherever chiefs' rule obtains in Africa no beggars and hungry have raised the cry to the very heavens for relief, [but] in our modern democracy the rich are few and the mourners for an opportunity to enjoy the blessings of the soil are myriad.[36]

Schomburg viewed democracy as an ideological facade. He argued that the political freedoms offered by America had no substance, no roots in actuality. In the land of freedom an elitist system actually ruled; a few had much and many had little. In Africa, by contrast, said Schomburg, the appearance of elitism had to be judged against the actual communitarian effect. Under "the patriarchal mode of paramount chiefs" no one went hungry and all had some say in what affected their lives.[37] In regard to the accuracy of these claims, Schomburg obviously viewed Africa through a somewhat romantic prism. For our purposes, it is enough to note that in citing evidence for the achievements of black culture, Schomburg did not point to only those black people or black institutions that most resembled the dominant Euro-American society. He also posed the possibility that in Africa and Asia people had developed ways of life that surpassed what the West offered, and that the claims of Western superiority and progress were only claims, with no basis in fact.

Schomburg suggested that some aspects of African culture involve different and, in some ways, more effective learning methods. To understand Africa as a foundation for black development in the Americas, it would be necessary not just to learn about the motherland but to learn as the African peoples do:

> We are reminded that the earliest instruction was imparted orally and this system is still found extant in Africa and among other Oriental nations. It is useful, because it trains the mind to list and retain. The modern school with its many books, but without systematic lectures, turns out many graduates who are lacking in retentiveness and no

sooner than the sound of the words has left their teachers'
lips, the subject has been forgotten; and if they are called
upon to explain the theme, it is reduced to an incom-
prehensible mass of meaningless words. The university
graduate is wont to overestimate his ability, fresh from
the machinery that endows him with a parchment and
crowns him with knowledge, he steps out into the world
to meet the practical men with years of experience and
mother wit. It is a contrast, the professional man with the
veneer of high art, and the acquaintance with the best
authors, and up to date histories demanding recognition.
All these books take their proper places when applied to
the white people, but when applied or measured up to
the black people, they lack the substantial and the inspir-
ing. They are like meat without salt, they bear no analogy
to our own; and for this reason it would be a wise plan
for us to lay down a course of study in Negro History and
achievements. . . .[38]

There are important and typical features in this piece.
Schomburg argued that oral tradition as a way of trans-
mitting knowledge was superior to the modern Western
ways of learning. These so-called modern methods produced, Schomburg said, a glibness, a superficial display of
learning, that is in reality a mere veneer. In contrast, the
oral traditions of Africa and "the Orient" required a sharp-
ening of the mind, a development of the intellect that was
more effective than university instruction. Schomburg was
not arguing that the oral should replace the written. Certainly Schomburg, the consummate bibliophile, was a firm
believer in the printed word. His emphasis here on the oral
and its virtues demonstrates his respect for what the people
as a group have created, in contrast to the products of single
intellectuals.

Schomburg went counter to the assumption that there
were universal objective methods of scientific inquiry. By
suggesting that comprehension of the oral tradition required
immersion in it, Schomburg implied that scholars limited
by Western training would be unable to analyze Africa. The
"darkness" of the impenetrable African continent takes on a
different and positive meaning here. Africa will be opaque

to all those who approach it from outside. Only through respecting the African frame of knowledge and learning within it could any real understanding take place. The difficulty with most scholarship on Africa was not just the racist assumptions of the scholars. Because they were blind to the intrinsic worth of African forms of life, these outsiders could not peer inward: they could not see the true Africa. Committed black scholars, then, would have to incorporate non-Western methods of learning and thought. In disdaining the veneer of "high art" and those who judge intellect on "mere acquaintance with the best authors," Schomburg opposed the notion that Euro-American intellectual traditions were universal. What Europe produced was European, what the Africans had produced was African.

Schomburg proposed seeing the West, Africa, and Asia in a specific historical context. His proposals were part of Schomburg's larger argument. He saw the domain of ideas as a major battleground in the struggle against oppression. On this ground of idealistic battle, history was an important tool in the march against subordination. Schomburg wrote:

> The American Negro must remake his past in order to make his future. Though it is orthodox to think of America as one country where it is unnecessary to have a past, what is luxury for the nation as a whole becomes a prime social necessity for the Negro. For him, a group tradition must supply compensation for persecution, and pride of race the antidote for prejudice. History must restore what slavery took away, for it is the social damage of slavery that the present generations must repair and offset.[39]

The average black person would have to become the "most enthusiastic antiquarian of them all."

The suggestion that the black population must become antiquarians must be read with caution. This is a political rather than academic statement. It was true, said Schomburg, that the unveiling of a suppressed historic record was essential for the formation of group unity or "racial integrity" among black people. Yet mere knowledge of the African past and the American past would not be enough. This knowledge would have to become part of the living traditions of the people. Here we must return to Schomburg's arguments concerning oral methods of learning. History could not remain in the hands of racist scholars. But neither could history, to be politically useful, be simply an academic exercise in the hands of a few black scholars. Everyone in the black community would have to become a historian. Thus, history would no longer be just a discipline, a privileged domain of those trained in a particular skill; it would become the expression of the people. History would become tradition.

To accomplish this transformation of history into the tradition of the people would require a blending of the people's outrage and pain with the rigorous scholars' approach. Schomburg did not mean that history could be uncovered without determination and discipline. It was important, he pointed out, that the development of the people's history be not "mere propaganda"; rather, it would have to be "systematic and scientific." [40] The science he had in mind was not that of detached and distant observation. His science would of necessity involve the motivation of pain and the discipline of fact. For example, Schomburg observed that the slave narratives were overflowing with the emotion of those held in chains and those who had escaped bondage, yet they were no less valuable as depictions of their time:

> The slave narratives offer a vast field to select from; they represent a collection of facts mingled with pain. The anguish and the vissicitudes are related with candor and pathos. And yet there is much of invaluable use, pertaining to different states, telling of conditions to be found elsewhere. John Brown's narrative deals with slavery in Georgia, William Wells Brown with Kentucky and Missouri, whereas Frederick Douglass and Samuel Ringgold Ward deal with conditions in Maryland. Each one gives the different shading to the subject and portrays with remarkable fidelity the naked truth. [41]

At the same time, continued Schomburg, it was important that the needed analysis not be swept away by crude unthinking reactions to racism:

The blatant Caucasian racialist with his theories and assumptions of racial superiority and dominance has in turn bred his Ethiopian counterpart—the rash and rabid amateur who has glibly tried to prove half of the world's geniuses to have been Negroes and to trace the pedigree of nineteenth century Americans from the Queen of Sheba.[42]

The creation of a living history of the people would take place through analytical exposure of the naked truth by those who were driven by their just outrage. That they might each give different shadings to their accounts, that their facts would be mingled with cries of pain, would not detract from their work. Fundamentally, it was the pain that lay bare the truth. For Schomburg, there was no conflict between a "racially patriotic" motivation and a "rigorous analysis." "A racial motive remains," he wrote, "legitimately compatible with scientific method and aim." Consequently, the task of the black scholar was to set "himself against a reclaimed background, in a perspective that will give pride and self-respect ample scope, and make history yield for him the same values that the treasured past of any people affords."[43]

The term "scholar" had a dynamic and expansive quality for Schomburg. The process of "reclaiming" the background of black people would not stop at scholarly analysis. The knowledge gained would be part of the wider movement to galvanize the black population into a unified group. As history became tradition, the people would assume the role formerly reserved for specialist scholars. The distinctions between scholars and people would vanish as history and tradition merged.

Schomburg was nothing if not idealistic. He firmly declared the power of ideas to shape the world. The transformation of consciousness through politically motivated scientific scholarship would contribute to the formation of a group solidarity which would challenge Euro-American domination. This scholarship would provide "the spark of learning," which would "awaken the soul" of the people, knowledge of history would kindle "the torches that will inspire us to racial integrity," he wrote.[44] For Schomburg ideas had a basic quality that made them impervious to the more transitory forms of oppression. No matter how oppressive was a society, it could not outlast the truth of ideas:

> With such crucial truths to document and establish, an ounce of fact is worth a pound of controversy. . . . Assembled from the rapidly growing collections of the leading Negro book-collectors and research societies, there were in these cases, materials not only for the first true writing of Negro history, but for the rewriting of many important paragraphs of our common American history. Slow though it be, historical truth is no exception to the proverb.[45]

But Schomburg's idealistic emphasis was important precisely because of its practical connections with real action. Scholarly analysis could not be a mere chess game carried out in an ivory tower. Direct and tangible consequences flowed from the victory of one mode of thought over another. When information concerning black people was fragmentary and distorted, the race was weakened. With the analysis and illumination of black history, social cohesion would be enhanced. Schomburg's was a practical idealism in which consciousness became a force for social development.

The importance of ideas did not imply a specialized caste of black intellectuals. The creation of ideas could take place among the people at large, not just among scholars. Schomburg's belief in the fusion of history and tradition, scholars and folk, allowed him to declare, "We need in the coming dawn the man who will give us the background for our future, it matters not whether he comes from the cloisters of the university or from the rank and file of the fields."[46]

Nor did Schomburg stop with this basic assumption. In his most critically significant work, an unpublished and unstudied proposal for a book on Afro-American culinary traditions, he emphasized that the creative energies of the black intellectuals from the academic cloisters would have to be understood alongside the equally formative and creative strengths of the people from the fields. It is to this work of Schomburg's that we now turn.

Sometime during the 1920s, Schomburg began to prepare a book examining the complete tradition of Afro-American cooking. His work did not materialize beyond a short proposal. Yet within the pages of this untitled and heretofore unknown work is the essence of Schomburg's perspective on Afro-American culture, as well as the relationship of the black intellectuals to the people.

This book, wrote Schomburg, would have

to range at breakfast time, for example, from the hearty egg breads and sugar-baked apples of Virginia to brains in brown butter and batter cakes with borders of crisp black embroidery in the Blue Grass, on down to rice cakes and ineffable steeped coffee, cinnamon flavored chocolate and hot toddies served in the early hours behind the sun-streaked jalousies of the Vieux Carré in New Orleans.[47]

The main divisions were to be based not on meat versus vegetable, on hot versus cold, or on sweet versus sour, but on the rhythm of the workday. On this foundation, Schomburg then proceeded in his characteristic way. He described a wide range of meals over an equally wide geographic area, all of which suggested a well-developed and extensive body of cooking styles.

This sense of black cooking as both a wide-ranging product of many people and as an identifiable creation of particular individuals was one of the basic dichotomies in his proposal. Schomburg named many "famous cooks"

from Dumas père who swore that he was born to be a cook—and proved it many times at the Sunday night suppers which he used to cook for his fellow-literateurs of France—to Black Dan, proprietor of Francues Tavern who might well be called the culinary father of American independence—since it was as Frederic J. Haskins once put it—"under Black Sam's roof and over Black Sam's excellent canvasback duck and venison haunch and Canaray and Madier and musty ale that the plans were discussed and fomented which ultimately resulted in the United States of America.[48]

Schomburg furthermore sought to

include personality sketches of many other famous Negro cooks—past and present—and many of their best receipts —a great many of which have never been published— such a one for instance as the formula for preparing terrapin practiced by a Washington cook who always invented some excuse for clearing the kitchen at the crucial moment and never revealed her magic. . . .

Schomburg went beyond a mere listing of famous cooks. The totality of black cooking was, for him, in the hands of many who cannot be named, who lived their lives in the privacy of their own homes, yet who were linked in a shared tradition of cooking skills. He sought "to show that the well-known colored cooks are exceptional partly because their names are known whereas the true creative impulse in cooking as in all folk arts is vested in anonymous thousands." For Schomburg, it was important to recognize cooking not as an empty set of written formulas but as the product of people. To the extent that they could be named, the cooks would be described individually in order to bring life to the general phenomenon. At the same time, there would be presented the image of a great stream of knowledge being transmitted over generations of relatives and friends, a stream of knowledge that did not depend upon a few famous individuals as its wellspring.

To understand black cooking, consequently, required more than ferreting out the histories of particular and noted individuals. A fully-developed analysis of black cooking would involve mingling with the people, "anonymous thousands." Schomburg, for example, learned the famous and mysterious recipe for terrapin not from the cook, who had kept the secret to herself, but from her daughter. The cook, said Schomburg, had revealed the formula only "on her deathbed to an only daughter—who has told it to us." Cooking among black people, Schomburg noted, involved "an unwritten cookbook" not found on bookstore or library shelves.[49]

As Schomburg described them, the significant dimensions of black cooking included the ceremonial, the symbolic, the economic, the African and West Indian, the relationship of rural to urban cooking, the importance of black cooking as a transformational means of resistence to racist domination, and, finally, the description of black cooking as a living tradition rather than a set of artifacts.

To understand how black cooks organized the occasions upon which food was served would, said Schomburg, expose important elements of black culture. It was important, said Schomburg,

to discourse whenever it seems appropriate upon the pomp and ceremonies attending the preparation and consumption of viands, of special dishes and beverages for special occasions such as egg-nog Rienna served on Christmas mornings and that mace-flavored oyster stew which is traditionally prepared for the annual St. Cecilia Ball in Charleston.[50]

And it would be necessary

to describe curious and most-forgotten customs in which feasting played some part—and most particularly the early New England elections of Negro governors and kings from among the slave populations of Connecticut and Rhode Island and of the Election cake and other delectables served at these feasts which often lasted through two days and nights.[51]

The cooking of food by black people is heavily infused with various layers of meaning, noted Schomburg. The recipes handed down are filled with numerous symbolic admonitions: "It is well known that an aged fowl is made tender by an iron nail and that all jellies, butter, sauce and soup must be stirred to the right, for otherwise they will not make. And that cake must be stirred clockwise."[52] In some cases, the link between cooking and religion is astonishingly direct. We must make a further study, he said, "of the religious background which must have inspired the famous Scripture cakes; the ingredients of which were listed by chapter and verse—such as three tablespoonfuls of Judges 11:8—honey. To reproduce the scriptural as well as a more workable version."[53]

Schomburg described cooking among black people in the United States, looking at how, despite living in a harsh environment and circumscribed by cooking methods of European origin, they managed to construct their own culinary realities. Schomburg was also, however, alert to historic influences. He hoped

> to uncover if possible such traces of Africanisms which still persist in American dishes. To compare for instance, the delectable Fish Head Stew served to millionaire fishermen on [Georgia] Sea Islands with a slightly similar concoction prepared by the Djuka Negroes [of Surinam] among whom, I am told, the fish is eaten like corn on the cob and heads especially considered a delicacy; the bones being crunched audibly and with much gusto. In this connection the mention that okra—and buckra—are words of African origin—and to write of the noble tradition of okra-gumboes, especially those served straight from the cooking pot.[54]

All of these ceremonial, symbolic, and African elements in black cooking present a fertile terrain for investigation.

It was not surprising to Schomburg that novelists such as Lafcadio Hearne and Owen Wister had spoken of Afro-American food. Indeed, the study of the literary treatment of black cooking would have to be included in any overall analysis. We must, he said, "recall other and more literary works about certain of the Negro cooks chef d'oeuvres—Owen Wister's dissertation in praise of Lady Baltimore cake, the Hergesheimer rhapsodies, Lafcadio Hearne's essays in praise of Creole cookery and other literary references."[55]

But, cautioned Schomburg, it would be a mistake to transfer the discussion of black cooking fully into a literary domain. This was not simply a world of happy creative black cooks busily preparing flavorsome meals. It was, rather, a brutal environment of poverty, of subordination, and sometimes of starvation. What black people cooked for white people was in some important ways distinct from what they cooked for themselves, and much of that had to do with oppression. We must, he wrote, retain in spite of poetry, a feeling for the grim economics which have influenced the Negro's choice of his own viands. To remember that in all communities the cheapest foods have been his staples—that crawfish and catfish and mustard green along with molasses, cornmeal, pork, beans and rice were not by accident—the backbone of his diet. That the cornmeal and pork psychosis to which Forest refers—has been literally forced down his throat.[56]

This oppressive reality meant that black people employed as cooks created two different styles of food, one for the whites, the other for themselves. According to Schomburg: "Negro cooking has developed along two lines—cabin cooking and cooking for the big house."[57] Such divisions, Schomburg indicated, had resulted in two parallel forms of cooking. It would be necessary to "remark upon the Negro's preference for his own flavory dishes as contrasted with the more elaborate ones which he prepares in his masters' kitchens." Nonetheless, a significant aspect for Schomburg was that the cooking, whether done in cabin or big house, was by black cooks. Southern cooking was Afro-American cooking. His culinary analysis would explain why "the Negro has always done the cooking in the South."[58] Schomburg here anticipated and overturned the oft-heard remark among Southern whites that "soul-food" was simply Southern food. To the contrary, said Schomburg, Southern food was black food.

For Schomburg, the remarkable feature of black cooking was that its creators had accomplished the task of subverting and converting the food of oppression into the staff of life. Black cooks, had taken the "psychosis of pork" and the European forms of cooking and had turned them into a positive and distinctive part of their own existences. This transformation was two-fold: a rejection of confinement within poor-folks food and a rejection of European dominance. "Somehow," wrote Schomburg, black people had "invented dishes to take the bad taste of charity away from the victuals doled out by relief committees in places like Detroit, for example."[59] Similarly, it was crucial to understand

how the Negro genius has adapted the English, French, Spanish and Colonial receipts taught him by his masters

just as he adapted the stern Methodist hymns and the
dour tenets of Protestantism—to his own temperamental
needs: and how he has modified them to express his own
peculiar artistic powers.[60]

Under the most trying and pervasively oppressive conditions, ranging from the plantation to the city relief line,
black people have managed, said Schomburg, not simply to
survive at the bare fringe of life but to infuse life into the
alien forms alotted them. In so doing, black people have
done more than survive through their cooking; they have triumphed. They have taken little and made it into much. They
have also created, through cooking, a distinctive boundary
between them and white America. The culinary synthesis
was unique. The various elements of black cooking realized
the genius and the distinctiveness of black people.

For Schomburg, the boundary established by the black
culinary arts was a demarcator of something autonomous in
Afro-American life. They represented a system of knowledge, a system known only to black people. Recipes were
part of the "unwritten Negro cookbook," a phrase that re-
ferred, in part, to an oral tradition. But more strictly, it
resembled an underground form of written communication,
a *samizdat*-type of sharing of recipes from hand to hand.
Underlying this exchange was a shared understanding of
coded signs, such as iron nails for tender chicken. This culinary system was highly fluid and required a social intimacy
that could not be expressed on the printed page:

> The exact formula for any but the most ordinary dishes
> cannot be written down—that a pinch of this and a hand-
> ful of that may be more excessive than level tablespoon-
> fuls in giving the feel of a dish. That no matter how
> ingredients are measured they must be combined with a
> sort of magic in order to achieve the perfect blend. That
> accurate oven thermometers and scientific renditions of
> certain inspired dishes are no more like the original than
> a photograph copy is like a Rembrandt. That it takes
> more—and less—than a knowledge of dietetics to make
> a cook.[61]

In this way Afro-American cooking proved intractable to scientific reduction and so resisted domination by the dominant culture.

This resiliency of Afro-American cooking was central to Schomburg's proposal. He was extremely careful not to reduce his proposal to a suggestion for folkloric gathering of dead or dying cultural forms. His was not a search for last remnants of vanishing peoples.[62] Certainly, there were dimensions of Afro-American cooking, such as the election cakes of Connecticut and Rhode Island during slavery, which were known only to historians interested enough to discover them. For Schomburg, however, such lost or obscure elements testified to the sound and long-lived foundation upon which the whole body of black cooking rests. That body of cooking was itself alive and well, he argued. It was a dynamic phenomenon constantly in the process of complex transformations as black people interacted with their own oppression and their own history.

Consequently, Schomburg did not restrict his proposed survey to the rural South. Rather, he drew a continuous line from there to the urban centers of the North. The black people who migrated to the North did not destroy an agrarian tradition but instead continued and developed it. In Harlem, said Schomburg, a vital melange of elements is bubbling under the direction of black cooks:

> Picture the teeming tropical markets in Harlem—exoticism under the El—canned flying fish to be had at 116th St. And of the rattlesnakes caught by Negro youths in Florida swamps and sold in glass jars by Park and Tilford. To tell how from the dingly flats in West Indian sections of Harlem—there comes early in October an odorous wave of Christmas fruit cake flavored with Haitian rum, brandy, wine, and rare tropical spices.[63]

Thus Schomburg saw no major cleavage between the rural south and the urban north. There was instead, he argued, a continuous current that made up the living tradition of black cooking. Significantly, this urban manifestation of culinary tradition was taking place primarily in the homes of black people rather than in restaurants. It was over the domestic stove that both the continuity and evolution of black culinary arts was occurring. We must admit, said Schomburg, "the non-existence of any first-class Negro restaurant in Harlem and . . . analyze the social and economic factors which made the colored people home eaters."[64]

Characteristically, Schomburg presented the difficult economic reality of black existence. He did not elaborate on the "social and economic factors" that make the operation of a successful black restaurant difficult, but they are not hard to imagine. Also characteristically, Schomburg refused to describe these economic realities in strictly negative terms. If the culinary tradition remained in the home, out of social and economic necessity, it also remained a dynamic part of a living history. It was at the hands of the "anonymous thousands," said Schomburg that the knowledge of Afro-American cooking was constantly being positively developed.

There are numerous pungent possibilities for further research in Schomburg's proposal. The Bible cakes with their scripture-coded recipes suggest a potentially important taxonomy of food and religion. The election feasts among black people in colonial New England, similarly, suggest an aspect of American and Afro-American history in need of more discussion. A comparison of African and Afro-American food preparation would be worthy of a volume.

Beyond these aspects, however, Schomburg saw black American cooking as an important indicator of cultural resistance to domination. The control of a people's food, the outside restrictions upon when, where, and how the people shall eat, are important means of domination of one group by another (as in the regimen of the prison or the military). That black people, limited by poverty and by alien cultural dictates, could transmute the available foods into their own product is, therefore, vitally important.

There is another element in Schomburg's focus on cooking. Food is at once a necessity and a pleasure. Food is a basis of conviviality, a solace in times of sorrow, a respite from hard toil. For black people to control the making of food became the basis for a spiritually liberated space within which the oppressive weight of the white world could be put aside. "Give me a pigfoot and a bottle of gin and I'll do the shimmy shammy til the daylight come," Bessie Smith sang.[65] Food, vital to the body and the soul, was no small matter in the great scheme of things. To lose control of food was to endanger one's very existence as well as to reduce the possibility of pleasure and support.

Schomburg's analysis of food preparation represents a critical reflection on an integral part of black culture. When we contrast Schomburg's position with the Vanguard perspective on folk-culture of Alain Locke and Charles Johnson in *The New Negro*, we immediately see the critical significance of Schomburg's work. At every crucial point, Schomburg's proposal for the study of Afro-American cooking provides a basis for a critique of Locke's and Johnson's assertions that only the "talented few" could abstract value from the creations of the folk. Schomburg shows that whether or not the intellectuals investigated black American cooking, that body of knowledge would continue to develop as it has for several hundred years. This knowledge was not in the hands of an exclusive set of specialists; it was fundamentally a domestic phenomenon.

The chasm between rural and urban, between past and present, was exposed as a false division, a misleading antagonism. In its place, Schomburg adduced continuity. He rejected the claim that folk culture is fragile, a phenomenon vanishing in the industrial age. Instead, Schomburg pointed to the durability of the people's culture, a strength that continues through slavery and through industrialism. The image of the intellectual's role as savior and transformer of tenuous folk culture is overthrown. The people were not raw and unformed in this cultural product. For black cooking there could be no Lockean transformation from folk art to fine art, for this art of the folk was already fine.

In Locke's understanding, the task of the black intellectuals was to provide a worldview within which the masses could develop a conscious understanding of their worth. *The New Negro* saw the rapidly urbanizing black population as even more susceptible to racist manipulation, even more prey to self-denigration. It would lack the cultural stamina to recognize the value of the past. The black intellectuals, culturally conscious and historically alert, would have to play the necessary vanguard role.

Schomburg shows the problem of Afro-American culture in a different light. The people had, on their own, bridged the gaps caused by slavery and urbanization; they had constructed a body of knowledge historically rooted yet flexibly receptive to changing times and places. In constructing this knowledge, black people had formed an important means of communality and group identity that served as a bulwark against subordination to the politically dominant society. As a product of the home, as a creation of the people, Afro-American cooking was resistant to cultural absorption. As a living knowledge, moreover, it was still functioning in the hands of its creators. Afro-American cooking could not be seen as a lost or dying phenomenon.

Schomburg's analysis of cooking can be applied to other important Afro-American institutions. The blues, for example, has its origins in the largely rural South. Its movement as a musical form to the urban centers such as Kansas City, Chicago, and Detroit produced a distinctive transformation known as the urban blues. The electrification of the guitar wrought important innovations on the older rural form. Just as cooking takes on new urban features, so does this music. Yet there is no absolute break between rural and urban. Many of the urban blues musicians are Southern-born. There is a constant influx of people from the South as well as a cross-circulating movement of people who play both in the cities and the towns. Recordings make the sounds of the city available in the countryside. Clearly, the urban environment shapes the distinctive sounds of the South Side Chicago blues. Yet, equally clearly, the urban blues in its form, its content, and its players is not traumatically divorced from its rural origins. Instead, there is a living bond between South and North embodied in those who play and those who listen.

The same is true for the black church. It is in the city that groups such as the Black Hebrews, Father Divine, and Daddy Grace thrived in a way that they could not in the more restrictive environment of the South. Yet churches such as the National Baptist Convention, U.S.A., the African Methodist Episcopal Church, and the African Methodist Episcopal Zion Church are not confined to either North or South, rural or urban. Their organization stretches across those divisions. Sharing modes of expression, circulating ministers and congregants from one area to another, these churches are characterized by cross-regional unity rather than by division based on geography or economics. This is not to say that a powerful organization like the Abyssinian Baptist Church in Harlem, which produced the influential Powell family of ministers, does not owe some of its size and influence to its location in New York City. Yet, as a Baptist church, Abyssinian is linked to thousands of other Baptist churches from the Mississippi Delta to the North. We can, as Schomburg advises, recognize the differing realities of the rural and urban settings and simultaneously note the continuities that run through them.

Schomburg's analysis of the rural-Southern, urban-Northern continuity is a pivotal critique of the general tendency to see great differences between city and country. Some of the major modern figures in urban analysis—like Robert Park; Louis Wirth, whose essay on urbanization has focused much contemporary research; and E. Franklin Frazier, who analyzed the disorganizing effects of the city on the black family—imputed great transformational powers to the urban environment.[66] In contrast, Schomburg emphasizes the transformational powers *of people* in differing environments. Black people do not simply become different as the social stimuli change. On the contrary: for Schomburg, the black community manages to retain key features of the non-urban world. Rather than being passively shaped by the city, people filter and transform its effects to create their own ways of life.

Schomburg's formulation of the rural-urban continuity is concrete, specific, and dynamically clear. His is no mushy view of a solidly compacted social whole in which there are no differences. He tells us very directly about the distinctions between different regions. In his description of "rattlesnakes under the El" in Harlem, Harlem does not become the South yet Harlem is not cut off from the South.

It is his ability to imagine both continuity and difference that marks the dialectic of Schomburg's work and separates him from those who simply categorize rural and urban as separate compartments.

For Schomburg, then, the task of intellectuals cannot be to create form where there is none or to systematize what Locke called the "raw energy" of the people. Rather, it is to illuminate the very intricacy and strength of the people's creations. But who benefits from such illumination? First and foremost, it is the intellectuals themselves. Adrift from the folk, the intellectuals can reduce their alienation from their people and so counteract their own subordination to the wider society. The very act of analyzing and portraying Afro-American culture is an important step in the growth of politically engaged and critically conscious intellectuals.[67]

The information uncovered by the intellectuals and the analysis they make may also actually be of some use to the people. To the degree that scholarly analysis can fuse with the people's understandings, the intellectuals may join with the broader population as contributors to the common work of developing and strengthening Afro-American culture. Through Schomburg, we thus arrive at a position that neither takes an anti-intellectual stance nor adopts an elitist emphasis. If the searchers and describers of Afro-American culture become pretentious and assume that without their activity the people are lost, they lose sight of the stubborn resilience that the black population has developed in the face of adversity. The people will keep on keeping on regardless, whether the intellectuals write or the artists paint. But if scholars and artists provide generally useful information and perspectives that can be shared and distributed, then their work is important.

For Schomburg, the culinary knowledge of black America was emblematic of the basic strength and continuity of Afro-American culture itself. The analysis could not stop with cooking. The fundamental form and movement of Afro-American culture would have to be clarified in all its dynamic intricate webbing. To do so, implied Schomburg, would expose the tough living core of creative resistance that had brought black people over the hills and valleys of tribulation and that would continue to sustain them in their journey.

The Universalization of Mutuality

The great limitation in the work of Ellis and Schomburg was the absence of any specific critical evaluation of the effect of capitalist development on black America. Although Ellis was especially concerned with the role of science and technology, he did not connect them overtly to capitalism. The issue of class relations both within the black population and with white workers and the white bourgeoisie also was not directly addressed. Consequently, there was no equivalent in the work of Ellis and Schomburg, to Du Bois's astute critique of white worker collaboration with colonialism in his "African Roots of the War."

Nevertheless, their underlying arguments about the interrelatedness of various elements of society pointed to a resolution of the dispute over whether the materialistic or idealistic domain of action was more important. Ellis and Schomburg pointed to a synthesis of the materialistic and idealistic arguments and to the simultaneity of cultural, economic, political, and social action.

Schomburg and Ellis developed a Mutualistic approach in their written work. It was left to the massive Universal Negro Improvement Association, in which Marcus Garvey played a prominent role, to put Mutuality into action on a global scale.

Marcus Garvey was born in Jamaica, but it was from Harlem in the 1920s that he worked, with others, to organize the Universal Negro Improvement Association and African Communities League (the phrase, African Communities League, was later dropped from the name). The UNIA has been much discussed and intense controversy still swirls around it. A number of writers including Tony Martin, J. A. Cronon, and others have provided excellent historic analyses of the UNIA.[68] Here I want briefly to point to the Mutualistic qualities of that movement.

The UNIA addressed itself to the conditions of oppression

and struggle for justice that faced all black people, not only in the new world but also in Africa, Europe, and even the Pacific. Black people, said Garvey, have a "common cause." Consequently, he declared, "I know no national boundary where the Negro is concerned." The UNIA was loyal to no existing nation: "The UNIA seeks," he wrote, "independence of government."[69]

This "common cause" was not merely opposition to racism. To the contrary, the movement sought a variety of grounds for unity through its highly organized communications among various federated chapters around the world. As Garvey wrote:

> The Universal Negro Improvement Association is a movement that seeks unlimited racial union and cooperation. We desire to draw humanity closer together than we have been before, for we realize that with East pulling against West, North pulling against South, there will be nothing left to us but utter ruin.
>
> We can well imagine ourselves as one great united people, having one aim, believing in one God, and having one destiny. To see four hundred million of us standing together as one man is the desire of us who lead the Universal Negro Improvement Association.[70]

The movement's newspapers were one means by which the struggle for freedom was waged: "We need crusaders in journalism who will risk everything for the promotion of racial pride, self-respect, love and integrity."[71] Garvey waxed enthusiastic about the efforts of the various UNIA newspapers, especially the *Negro World*, which was distributed in Spanish and English language editions throughout North and South America, the Caribbean, Africa, and Europe.

Tony Martin observes that the *Negro World* was distributed throughout Africa, where it "was translated into scores of dialects [or languages] twenty-four hours after arrival and carried by fleet runners into the hinterland, up the great lakes of Southeast Africa." Simultaneously, it was being distributed in Chicago and New York, down the Mississippi Delta, and in Havana. Martin notes, "The *Negro World* penetrated every area where black folk lived and had regular readers as far away as Australia. It was cited by colonial powers as a factor in uprisings and unrest in such diverse places as Dahomy, British Honduras, Kenya, Trinidad, and Cuba."[72] The powers-that-be often blame indigenous rebellion on outside forces and so the *Negro World* may not have been so effective as the citations imply. Nonetheless, the paper's call for black independence and for unity of all black people did indeed cause well-documented concern in numerous colonial offices.

In addition to the *Negro World*, the UNIA published a number of other papers, including *La Nacion, La Prensa,* and *African World* (in South Africa). It is indicative of the ecumenical quality of the UNIA that differences in language and culture were in no way seen as a barrier to black unity across the northern and southern hemispheres. Instead, as in Schomburg's analysis, the African-American continuities cutting across those lines were emphasized.

The emphasis on shared consciousness through *The Negro World* and other newspapers was only part of the Mutualistic approach employed by the UNIA. According to Garvey, "We need improvement in every line—socially, religiously, industrially, educationally, and politically. We need the creation of a common standard among ourselves."[73] Religion was important, but Garvey wrote, "I am not one of those Christians who believe that the Bible can solve all the problems of humanity."[74] There also had to be "economic and industrial independence."[75] Nevertheless, for those who found religion important, the UNIA welcomed black Christians, Muslims, and Jews:

> Every individual or sect should be allowed to serve God according to the dictates of their own conscience. No race or country has the right to control the religious faith of its members or citizens; this is a very delicate subject and one that [we] should try to deal very cautiously with, lest we create dissension or breaches in the race that will take years to mend if at all.[76]

Thus, the UNIA included diverse modes of religious belief under the umbrella of the organization.

The UNIA's effort to develop industry was a clear echo of Booker T. Washington's hope of "materializing" the race through economic development. But unlike Washington's single-minded focus on economic power, such development was to be coupled with a revolution in culture and consciousness. Garvey was emphatic on the significance of black history: "The white world," he wrote, "has always tried to rob and discredit us of our history."[77] For those who understood the great achievements of black people, an entirely different historical pictured emerged. The act of understanding the real African past was viewed as a move toward the future. If black people had been ascendent once, they could be so again. It was for this reason, Garvey argued, that whites resorted to "every means to keep Negroes in ignorance of their history."[78] History was important not simply as a corrective record but as evidence of deep potential for change— evidence that could give support for peoples' social action. Historical knowledge could further present action.

For the UNIA, economic development, historical knowledge, socially engaged religion, and journalism were equally valid among many domains of action. In line with this emphasis, the UNIA was staunchly pro-local and anti-parochial. It drew from a wide variety of local populations but it made no distinctions of superiority on the basis of language, religion, or special skills. The diffusion of the UNIA newspapers to many localities reflected the diversity of its membership. For example, the UNIA chapter in Cuba played an important role as a defender of Haitian and Jamaican sugar cane workers in that country. The UNIA was especially strong in South Africa where migrant West Indian longshoremen worked on the docks. There were UNIA chapters in the Caribbean, Venezuela, Mexico, Guatemala, Brazil, West Africa, England, and Wales. In the United States the UNIA was not restricted to northern cities, finding extensive support in rural areas of Georgia, Mississippi, Alabama, and Arkansas. Drawing no distinctions between rural and urban Muslims or Christians, intellectuals or workers, the UNIA positioned itself as the organization of "one mighty race."

But it was the people who were mighty and not the

leaders. The UNIA was critical of authoritarian hierarchical power. Although the UNIA certainly celebrated the trappings of leadership, it spoke against black people who sought merely to continue modes of inequality:

> The Negro has had enough of this vaunted practice of race superiority as inflicted upon him by others. Therefore he is not prepared to tolerate a similar assumption on the part of his own people. . . . We desire to help them to build up Africa as a negro Empire, where every black man, whether he was born in Africa or in the Western world, will have the opportunity to develop on his own lines under the protection of the most favorable democratic institutions.[79]

There would be leadership, but it would be accountable to the people. It would not privilege a particular group; rather, it would be drawn from the entire spectrum of black people.

Never before had there been an organization that tied together black Mexicans, South African mine workers, Jamaican cane cutters, and Harlem working people in such a direct and concrete way. There was no mystical appeal to a vague common heritage, no cult of the past. By joining a UNIA chapter, a person immediately became part of a world-circling organization. At the same time, each chapter was local and responsive to its particular circumstances.

Garvey is often described (or criticized, depending on the observer's perspective) as being anti-intellectual. Indeed, Garvey fought bitterly with people like W. E. B. Du Bois and the *Messenger* socialists who often described him as a buffoon. Some historians have suggested that Garvey was rejected by the black intelligentsia. In fact, the broadly inclusive UNIA had cooperative relationships with a number of middle-class intellectuals.[80] Their contributions to the growth of the UNIA were especially pronounced in the field of history. Since the UNIA did not denigrate analysis or the pursuit of knowledge but saw such activities as a vital dimension of action, it would have been out of character for them to exclude intellectuals. Among those whose contributions were welcomed were Arturo Schomburg; Carter G. Woodson, the founder of the Association for the Study of

Negro History; William Ferris, who served as editor of the *Negro World*; J. A. Rodgers, an important disseminator of historic facts whose columns appeared in most black newspapers; Marie Du Chatellier of Panama; and John Bruce, a prolific New York writer and staunch defender of the UNIA.

Garvey did not reject intellectuals as such. Rather, like Booker T. Washington, Garvey was suspicious of Westernized black elites concerned more with their own refinement than with the struggle for freedom. Intellectuals who were willing to work for and within the UNIA were welcomed, but the organization was not top heavy with them. From the local chapters up through the divisions, everyday black people managed the affairs of the association in all its far-flung locations. At its peak, the UNIA is estimated to have had over one million members. Even those most critical of the UNIA had to admit to its popular base. The UNIA was clearly a mass movement. C. L. R. James points out that by "1920 the UNIA was proportionately the most powerful mass movement in America."[81]

The UNIA also gave its support to other anti-colonial struggles. Garvey sent a congratulatory telegram to DeValera of the Irish Republic and declared the UNIA to be a part of world-wide battles for freedom from Africa, Ireland, India, and Russia to the Americas. In its Mutualistic fashion, the UNIA celebrated its own distinctiveness as a black movement while proclaiming its affinities with other movements among different peoples.

It is indicative that the UNIA newspaper, the *Negro World*, was the only source of pro-Nicaraguian news available to people in that country during the 1927–1932 resistance to U.S. intervention there. Ted Vincent points out how the *Negro World* condemned that intervention, declaring that the Marines were "killing white men and black in Nicaragua."[82] In offering support to Sandino and his guerillas, the UNIA did not depart from its mission. On the contrary it was from their own distinctive sense of identity that the organization embraced others who were resisting exploitation, no matter what their color or where they were fighting.

In sum, the Universal Negro Improvement Association

cut across a wide variety of geographic, linguistic, religious, national, and racial boundaries. Internally, it valorized both the materialistic-economic and idealistic-cultural domains. Group consciousness was viewed as crucial to successful economic development, just as economic development was seen as vital to group consciousness. The UNIA did not identify one dominant central domain or look for an elite cadre to lead the vast unknowing masses. Instead it affirmed that black people had conscious creative capabilities that would sustain the organization that they, in all their rich global diversity, were creating. Moreover, the organization had so strong a sense of its own particular identity and objectives that it offered support to other struggles for freedom. The Universal Negro Improvement Association was an organizational embodiment of the possibility of Mutuality.

Clearly, the UNIA was more than the skills and leadership of Marcus Garvey. Unhappily, much of the debate has focused so much on him that the impressive grass-roots reality of the UNIA has been obscured. Ironically, this Mutualistic organization par excellence is often misrepresented by considering it as merely the creation of one man. The rebuttal of the Vanguard perspective implied in the very existence of the UNIA has usually been ignored. Unfortunately, the UNIA bears some responsibility for this state of affairs. A major weakness of the organization was its tendency to glorify Garvey, to construct around him what would now be called a cult of personality thus blunting peoples' recognition of their major role in the building of the UNIA.

Nonetheless, the basic cornerstone of Vanguard perspective claims to legitimacy—namely, the supposed backwardness of the isolated, unconscious, and inchoate masses was fundamentally challenged by the very existence of the Universal Negro Improvement Association. It was little wonder that the organization was attacked by Vanguardists who put aside their differences to put down the stern challenge of a non-Vanguard approach to the world.

The UNIA's Mutualistic approaches indicated that black people around the world were alert to one another's needs and to other struggles for freedom. The UNIA demonstrated what millions of everyday people in diverse locales could accomplish when they were linked to parallel developments around the world. The multi-dimensional organization showed the way for a Mutualistic focus on many domains of struggle, from the economic to the cultural, and on many communities of people with many perspectives.

5

From the 1960s into the Future

Can we make sense of the last few decades using the concepts of Vanguard perspective and Mutuality? I believe they can be of significant usefulness in understanding groups as diverse as the Nation of Islam and the Student Non-Violent Coordinating Committee, writers such as Harold Cruse and Ralph Ellison, as well as aspects of music and the arts.

The Vanguard Perspective

One of the most important organizational examples of a tendency toward the Vanguard perspective can be found in the Nation of Islam during the 1960s. Founded in the 1930s by Wallace D. Fard and brought to its organizational strength through the leadership of the Honorable Elijah Muhammad, the Nation has a deserved reputation for its success in attracting and aiding those cast off by society. The Nation helped former prisoners, the downtrodden and the alienated, to achieve a sense of dignity and discipline. But, despite its appeal to the masses, the Nation of Islam was oriented toward the Vanguard perspective.

Where the Universal Negro Improvement Association was inclusive, the Nation of Islam roundly condemned the black Christian churches. Its leader, Elijah Muhammad, called Christianity a "slave religion" that had first been forced on black people and then had been accepted by

them. In accepting the religion of their oppressors, black
people contributed to their own oppression.

> The American so-called Negroes are gravely deceived
> by the slave-master's teaching of God. . . . They do not
> know they are deceived and earnestly believe they are
> right regardless of how vile the white race may be. . . .
> Christianity is one of the most perfect black-slave-making
> religions on our planet. It has completely killed the so-
> called Negroes' mentality.[1]

For Elijah Muhammad, Christianity was only one factor
in the subordination of an authentic black consciousness.
Black people, he asserted, had fallen prey to the intense
materialism of American society, to the lust for profit and
creature comforts. So powerful was this attraction that black
people had lost touch with themselves and each other. Black
people were "charmed by the luxury of their slave master,
and [could not] make up their minds to seek for self something of this good earth."[2] Instead of such seeking a healthy
existence, black people, deluded by the slave mentality that
their ancestors learned through Christianity, had become
"victims of drunkenness, drug addiction, reefer smoking . . .
in a false and futile attempt to 'escape' the reality and the
horror of the shameful condition that the Slavemasters' religion has placed us in. . . ."[3]
   Of interest to our discussion is the firm rejection of
everything associated with the contemporary condition of
black people in America. Muhammad did not attack white
churches but black churches such as the African Methodist Episcopal and the National Baptist Convention, U.S.A.
The black churches were the enemy because, as community institutions, they legitimized oppressive religion. Black
Christianity was portrayed as the opiate of the people alongside the real drugs of marijuana and heroin and the social
opiates of gambling and other vices. The Nation of Islam
admitted no viable positive Afro-American culture. All was
tainted. Afro-American culture was part of a "world floating
in corruption."[4]
   The broad black masses thus could not create, on their

own, revolutionary change. They were too infected by the degenerate society they were a part of, whether they were churchgoers or pimps. If the people could not extricate themselves from their bondage, what could be done?

There would have to be a complete rejection of American society. Muhammad proclaimed:

> Stop spending money for tobacco, dope, cigarettes, whisky, fine clothes, fine automobiles, expensive rugs and carpets, idleness, sport and gambling. Stop . . . living on credit loans . . . seeking the highest priced merchandise. . . . If you must have a car, buy the low-priced car.[5]

This sharp rejection could be accomplished only through a special knowledge, the knowledge of Islam. Islam, the "True Faith," was the opposite of Christianity, "the slave master's religion." Islam would awaken the people, open their eyes to the sordid reality around them, and provide the way to create a new world. Muhammad wrote:

> My poor people are mentally blind, deaf and dumb, and full of fear. Blind because they do not see the light of truth after being shown it for over thirty years. Deaf because they will not hear the truth. Islam that has come to them from Allah through the Messenger (myself).[6]

Those who had accepted Islam would be in a position to lead the mentally blind masses from their affliction. Who can be saved? asked Elijah Muhammad. The answer was, the Muslim believers.[7] Islam, Muhammad asserted, was the original religion of the black people before they became enslaved.

Thus the Nation of Islam claimed a special knowledge and portrayed itself as the directing group that would lead the people from their bondage. The people would not be able to do this themselves, for they had lost their original culture. Afro-Americans had been swept up in the culture of the oppressor without gaining anything of worth. For the Nation, the primary domain of action was religious consciousness. When that changed, all else would follow. But it was the Nation of Islam that would define religious consciousness.

Religious expressions that had grown up in the new world were to be rejected for approaches that were more purely "African."

The Nation's newspaper, *Muhammad Speaks*, scathingly attacked not only Afro-American Christianity but Afro-Brazilian and Haitian religions as well. Brazil's Candomblé religion, based on the Yoruba pantheon of the Gods, was denounced as "paganism." Vodun in Haiti was also repudiated.[8] In rejecting these unique expressions of Afro-American religion, this approach to black nationalism actually was rejecting the tangible ways in which people had maintained their ties with Africa in their daily lives. As C. L. R. James said of Haitian folk culture:

> Left to themselves, the Haitian peasantry resuscitated to a remarkable degree the lives they had lived in Africa. Their method of cultivation, their family relations and social practices, their drums, songs, and music, such art as they practised and above all their religion which became famous, Vodun—all this was Africa in the West Indies.[9]

Thus, it is a living transformation of African into new world forms that the Nation of Islam was attacking when it condemned Western Hemisphere practices as "pagan." Similarly, much cultural nationalism in the 1960s downplayed the indigenous Afro-American creativity displayed in forms such as music (the Delta, Piedmont, and Urban blues), quilting, and cooking, and turned to Africa for models of music, clothing, and food. Interestingly, this turning away from the living culture of Afro-Americans to a "rediscovery" of the lost past put the cultural nationalism of the 1960s close to the position of Alain Locke's Harlem *literati* in *The New Negro*.

Although the focus on re-inventing Africa neglects the actual African dimensions of New World black experience, this type of approach is generally the one taken within the Vanguard perspective. Culture is not the product of the people at large but rather is the domain of a conscious directing group. Culture cannot be an emanation of the living folk, for that would undercut the authority of the directing group. So Afro-Brazilian Candomblé, Afro-American Christianity, and the blues must be sidestepped because they are living expressions of the people's consciousness and so cannot be managed by one group claiming special knowledge. By denouncing Afro-American Christianity simply as "slave religion," the Nation did not leave much room for coalitions with black Christians. By its overall attack on existing Afro-American cultural forms, the Nation cut itself off from closer contacts with everyday people for whom that culture is a living reality. It is to the great credit of the Nation of Islam that it reached out to the downtrodden and the forgotten. Yet in doing so as a Vanguard group, the Nation thrust itself away from dynamic aspects of Afro-American life that are not negative and that need to be addressed and recognized as positive.

Similarly, the Black Panther Party (BPP) declared itself unabashedly "the Vanguard of the people" and, in its formative period, condemned all black religion as an instrument of oppression. Although the BPP drew from Leninist and Maoist models, much as the *Messenger* socialists drew from Bolshevism, both groups were squarely within the Vanguard perspective. They were not adapting ideas available to all from within a group situation. Rather, they were handing down a ready-made mode of social thought, which incorporated themselves as the leaders and arbiters.

We find another important example of this Vanguard thought in the work of the courageous George Jackson, assassinated by the authorities in Soledad Prison. He spoke about the asserted failure of the black family as an example of the general failure of Afro-American culture: "The black family unit is in ruins. It is our first and basic weakness." Jackson considered that the chance for cultural development among black people had been critically eroded: "Our culture, institutions, and customs, upon which unity depends and without which cohesiveness can never exist, were destroyed and never replaced."[10] Jackson downgraded the activities of women, saying that women are naturally "subservient."[11] He thus neglected the tremendous organizational potential of black women, whose achievements have been fundamental to both the black church (an institution also condemned by Jackson) and the community in general.

Like Booker T. Washington, Jackson held little brief for the black elite, seeing them as essentially imitative of their white counterparts. The black elite, he said, can do little more than "cling to a kind of subculture that manifests itself today in the hideous notion that if we educate ourselves properly, think the right thoughts, read the right books, say the right things, and do exactly what is expected of us—we can be as good as white people."[12] Both the educated elites and the broad masses of black people suffer from the same illusions. Black people in America live in an environment of pain that is clouded by the illusions of well-being: "We look at life through our rose-colored glasses, rationalizing and pretending that things are not so bad after all."[13]

For Jackson, there was no genuine Afro-American culture. That culture had been long-since obliterated through brute force. Whether it was educated black persons who seek to copy their oppressor, or street hustlers whose materialism was a carbon copy of Western habits, black people had traded their self-determination for "a car, cheap mass-produced clothes, a clapboard house, or a couple of nights a week at the go-go." To uproot this pervasive illusion was a monumental task, for black people had been "thoroughly terrorized, dehumanized, and divested of those things that from birth make men strong." Jackson's critique of the striving for material things echoed those of Du Bois and Washington. In many ways, his solution paralleled the Nation of Islam's, albeit in a secular way. Given the huge task of changing people's consciousness, he looked to a directing group: "Every mass movement in history has been led by one person or a small group of people. . . . The difference between successful and unsuccessful mass movements is the people who lead them." The people, "will come out of their coma," wrote Jackson, and when they do, "I want to be in the vanguard."[14] Once again, we find the familiar themes: the sleeping opiated people, the deluded elites, and the need for a directing group whose special knowledge, purity, and discipline is essential to bring about revolution in the corrupting environment.

Harold Cruse, whose classic work on culture and politics, *The Crisis of the Negro Intellectual*, is necessary reading for any student of Afro-American issues and cultural politics in general, moves in similar Vanguard directions. Cruse writes that the black intellectuals must direct the development of an autonomous Afro-American national movement. "The Program of Afro-American Nationalism," he writes, "must activate dynamism on all social fronts under the guidance and direction of the Negro intellectuals." The major problem confronting the political struggle of black people, asserts Cruse, is the lack of a "real functional corps of intellectuals to confront and deal perceptively with American realities on a level that social conditions demand."[15]

Cruse holds that the black intellectuals must exercise a leading role because of their control over one dominant domain—culture. "The special function of the Negro intellectual," he asserts, "is a cultural one." Culture is the dominant domain because it permeates all others: it "is deeply entwined with the roots of the political, economic, and societal foundations of American national structure." Thus, there can "be no real black revolution in the United States without the cultural revolution."[16]

For Cruse, it is vital that the black intellectuals carry out their vanguard role in culture because black people, like the American people in general, lack analytical understanding of the cultural framework in which they live: "The American people, aside from the handful of power wielders in the upper levels, have very little social control over the economic, class, and political forces of the American capitalist dynamic. They are in fact manipulated by them." Because the masses are manipulated, the elite with their intellectual understanding of culture must "learn how to control and channel such forces," in order to make revolutionary change.[17]

This brief survey indicates something quite interesting. From the Nation of Islam to Harold Cruse, we find a diverse group of approaches that have a common tendency toward the Vanguard perspective; that is to say, they lean in the same direction as the early Du Bois, the *Messenger*, the *New Negro*, and Booker T. Washington. All are alert to the degrading, corrosive effects of oppression on black people. All emphasize the need for disciplined elites to bring about action within the one dominant domain they have identified. The masses are helpless until they are led to effective resistance in this arena of greatest opportunity. People like George Jackson, who knew ghetto life first-hand, concur here with the *New Negro* literati and with the intellectualist approaches of Cruse and Du Bois. They all focus strongly on the degrading effects of oppression and do not take full account of the achievements of people who historically have survived and subverted that oppression. The Vanguard perceives itself as separate both from the degraded masses and from the degrading environment. This sense of living in a distinctively separate zone gives the Vanguard its powerful sense of purity. This pure space could be occupied by Du Bois's humanistic elite, the Nation of Islam's disciplined Muslims, or the Black Panther cadres—all of whom sought to avoid the snares of the wider society. Yet this separation implied superiority over the unenlightened, who must be led out of their darkness.

Curiously, although the "class" focus of Marxism is usually thought to clash with the "race" focus of Afro-American nationalism, the two movements take similar approaches. They share a distrust of the indigenous consciousness of the people and a belief in the need for a vanguard directing group. Reference to the Vanguard perspective can reveal the shared assumptions of apparently conflicting movements —and also great differences between apparently similar groups.

Mutuality

Despite its seemingly elite organizers, the Student Non-Violent Coordinating Committee (SNCC) in its early days managed to follow a strongly Mutualistic approach in both practice and theory. Former SNCC organizer and sociologist Hardy Frye points out that organizing in oppressed Southern communities came about partly through the work of small cadres of urban activists. Joyce Ladner uses the term "cosmopolitans" to refer to this "intellectual elite" of "urban, educated, and highly skilled young people who were usually newcomers to the South."[18] Drawing on their outside experience and having a global perspective on the revolutionary changes occurring elsewhere in the world, this group brought with them a diverse set of skills. As Frye observes, "They were writers, musicians, painters, photographers, and their general orientation toward life and politics was an intellectual one." Their world outlook was well developed: "This group was . . . familiar with the history and writings of liberation struggles being carried on within the 'Third World.'" They saw the struggle in the South as similar to those other struggles: "For the cosmopolitans, the oppression of black people in the United States was comparable to that of 'people of color' throughout the neo-colonized world."[19]

At first glance, this cosmopolitan group would seem a clear example of a Vanguard elite. This is, however, a misperception that comes from associating politically engaged intellectuals with vanguard techniques. The key question, as should be evident at this point in our discussion, concerns the relationship of this group with the non-cosmopolitans, whom Ladner refers to as "locals." Frye's analysis indicates that the relationship was not one of leaders and led, nor was it marked by rejection of the creations of the people.

It is true, as Frye indicates, that SNCC's Black Power philosophy forced many locals (after many attempts to integrate into political power) to "question the effectiveness and wisdom of their traditional organizational tactics and goals."[20] Yet, in no way did the local people simply receive knowledge from the cosmopolitans. Rather, they took what was being offered, learned from it, and transformed their strategies. At the same time, their influence transformed the philosophy itself. They approached organizing, says Frye, in a pragmatic way that fit their circumstances: "The locals began to incorporate this new perspective into their political rhetoric and plans." Along with Black Power tactics, they "still adopted strategies using techniques that had survived from the integration era." Indeed, "though the locals now recognized the connection between liberation struggles on the national and international levels . . . they maintained [that] their immediate situation required working on the 'home front' first."[21]

The cosmopolitans contributed a philosophic perspective that had an important impact on the growth in "racial consciousness and black political activism" in the South. But as Frye says, "race and consciousness" already existed "in black communities, pervading most, if not all of black people's social, economic, and political behavior."[22] As Stokely Carmichael and Charles Hamilton point out:

> There were several black organizations in Lowndes County, all centered around the church: the Baptist ministerial alliances and the lodges. . . . All these groups met regularly, held functions, made decisions, collected and paid money—again laying bare the myth that black people were unorganized and unable to organize themselves.[23]

So the cosmopolitans did not create organization where there was none; they did not introduce political consciousness to the unconscious masses. Nor did they denigrate existing local black organization.[24] They *did* contribute a group of people having certain useful skills, and they introduced a political philosophy with global connections that became part of major changes in the South.

But if SNCC in its time exemplified the Mutuality approach in action, it also was prone to a weakness that characterized the Universal Negro Improvement Association. The Mutualistic tendencies in the organization tended to be overwhelmed by increasing emphasis upon individual leaders like Stokely Carmichael and H. Rap Brown. Furthermore the emergence of the Black Panther Party with its Vanguard attitude drew SNCC away from Mutuality and toward vanguard orientations as its top leadership sought to adapt to the rapidly changing political circumstances.[25] As happened with the UNIA, the tremendous creative accomplishment of working in productive egalitarian ways with local people tended to be lost in all the smoke of national revolutionary politics. This loss of emphasis on real Mutualistic success was abetted by the major news media, all of which are prone to look for "leaders" rather than to investigate more complex forms of mass mobilization. The typical media emphasis on elites rather than on grass roots obscured the achievements of large numbers of people.

Sadly, the same can be said for another Mutualistic experiment, that of Martin Luther King, Jr., and the Southern Christian Leadership Conference.

King's thinking on the limits of human knowledge incorporated a basic critique of Vanguard perspective positions that assume special knowledge held by a particular group. Having argued against the claims that certain groups have access to the absolute truth, King then went on to call for a more open and tolerant universe of political action among the oppressed. In this tolerant universe, many different positions would be attempted and respected. There would be both cohesion and variety. The imperative of toleration, which recognized the fact that no one group or person had the answer to oppression, required diversity within unity. King wrote: "This plea for unity is not a call for uniformity. There must always be healthy debate. There will be inevitable differences of opinion."[26] Because oppression took many complex and diverse forms, equally complex and diverse responses were called for. No one vantage point could command a view of the totality of oppression. Thus King advised, "The dilemma the Negro confronts is so complex and monumental that its solution of necessity involves a diversified approach."[27]

Nor did King's Mutualistic tendencies stop with an attack on the claim of special knowledge and a call for diverse approaches. Toleration of diversity would lead to mutual transformation as various groups came to recognize the roles that they could play. In this way, King argued both for participation of existing Afro-American organizations and for some modification of their approaches: "There are already structured forces in the Negro community that can serve as the basis for building a powerful united front—the Negro church, the Negro press, the Negro fraternities and sororities, and the Negro professional associations." But King went on to say, "We must admit that these forces have never given their full resources to the cause of Negro liberation. There are still too many Negro churches that are absorbed in a future good 'over yonder,' that they condition their members to adjust to the present evils 'over here.'" King then went on to use the same formula to describe other black organizations.

Note how different this approach was from the Vanguard thrust, even while it incorporated certain Vanguard-like criticisms of indigenous Afro-American culture. King criticized churches and secular institutions that had not played an active social role or had distracted people from social action. But he did not identify these organizations with the oppressive society as "slave religions" or the like. Rather he saw in these groups a source of resistance that could be mobilized with certain modifications in their organizational goals. King had an unfortunate tendency to overstate how little such groups had done, but he never descended into a broad attack on their basic integrity and cultural roots.

Also important for understanding King's Mutualistic tendencies is his emphasis on diversity not only of organizations but also of strategies. For example, King felt that although legal action had gained a great deal, it had overshadowed other approaches that non-specialists could undertake. He wrote, "When legal contests were the sole form of activity the ordinary Negro was involved as a passive spectator. His interest was stirred, but his energies were unemployed." In contrast, mass demonstrations and organizing offered everyday people a chance to play active roles in the struggle: "Mass marches transformed the common man into the star performer and engaged him in total commitment."[28] His emphasis on the common man as star performer marks another Mutualistic element in King's work. For King, mass action signified participatory action. It was important that all involved in social struggle develop as active participants through their cohesive cooperation with others.

Here King again touches on the element of transformation. Mass struggle transforms the common man into a star performer. The Vanguard sense of the people as inchoate energy to be directed by a few leaders is far from King's thought. Rather King saw self-transformation as inextricably intertwined with social transformation. Where, for example, the legalistic approach in isolation focused on only one aspect of multidimensional oppression and marginalized people by its reliance on specialists, King aimed for a broader approach incorporating many different strategies carried out by many people from all walks of life. People had to participate in their own liberation. Existing people's organizations such as the churches and sororal/fraternal organizations had to be drawn into the general struggle. The creativity of the people was a basic premise of King's social philosophy.

King did not desert his basic Mutualistic approach when he confronted those whose positions seemed to be diametrically opposed to his own. In particular, his relations with black nationalism and with groups that argued for armed resistance or armed revolution are instructive examples of how he moved to follow a Mutualistic approach with those who did not recognize Mutuality as a cohesive world view.

In his excellent work, *The Political Philosophy of Martin Luther King, Jr.*, Haynes Walton can find no fully developed strategy in King's thinking that provides a "basis by which to judge coalition arrangements."[29] Walton is quite right that King lacked a programatic method for establishing coalitions. Nonetheless, when viewed through the focus of Mutuality, King's work points to a philosophy of coalition.

King, in keeping with his drive toward toleration within the struggle, did not attack black separatism. To the contrary, he characteristically expressed his respect for the achievements of the Nation of Islam among the poor and dispossessed of the cities. Quite unlike the Nation's blanket condemnation of Afro-American Christianity, King's more Mutualistic tack lead him to look within black separatism for some common ground: "While I strongly disagree with their separatist black supremecy philosophy, I have nothing but admiration for what our Muslim brothers have done to rehabilitate ex-convicts, dope addicts, and men and women who, through despair and self-hatred, have sunk to moral degeneracy."[30]

King's admiration for Muslim success was a bridge between his Christianity and their Islam. He hinted that black Christians and Muslims had parallel concerns regarding materialism. Moreover, King's positive approach to the Muslims reflected a general tendency within black communities. Many black people deeply respected the Nation of Islam without themselves becoming Muslims. King's openness to a religion not his own was grounded in broad community realities.

Similarly, for all his disagreements with the advocates of "Black Power," King was willing to argue that "Black Power has a broad and positive meaning." It was a "call to black people to amass the political and economic strength to achieve their legitimate goals."[31] Here again King extended an open hand to those with whom he disagreed, some of whom considered him an Uncle Tom and apologist for the status quo. By focusing on the economic and political aspects of Black Power, King sought to find areas of common concern. He too believed that economic and political power was necessary.

Of course, no real alliances between King's part of the movement and black separatism developed. Instead there was a growing division. Although Walton observes that King's thought included no program for coalition building, the problem was somewhat deeper. King certainly had the necessary openness for a Mutualistic approach that could include many variations. A major problem, however, was the intransigence of Vanguard thinking. While King could advance toward common ground, Vanguard perspective groups such as the Nation of Islam and the Black Panther Party could not. At the very moment that King was suggesting overlapping concerns, nationalists and Marxists groups were attacking his tactics of passive resistence as too little, too late. It was not for lack of toleration or effort that King did not establish such coalitions. Walton himself notes that King's "position was far less inflexible than many, for he thought every alliance should be considered on its own merits."[32] It was Vanguard resistance to dialogue and coalition that led to increasing division, rather than a lack of detailed strategy on King's part. This point is important, for as long as the differences between the likes of King, the Nation of Islam, and black Marxists are described in concepts such as "conservative" and "radical," the underlying causes of these divisions will not be understood.

Finally, the expanded public persona of King did not contribute to his Mutualistic objectives. The recognition that many people played vital roles in actions such as the Montgomery bus boycott tended to be lost as attention was concentrated on King himself. Again recalling the UNIA experience, a cult of the personality diverted attention from the solid grass-roots achievements of everyday people. The recognition that so many people played such vital roles in actions such as the Montgomery bus boycott must be made clear so that people can withstand the temptation to take elite routes even though Mutualistic approaches have borne great fruit. The analysis of Mutuality, while certainly useful for scholarly understandings of Afro-American social thought, is also crucial if this egalitarian world view is to be armored against usurption by Vanguard perspective thinking.

Let us now consider another example of Mutuality in Afro-American social thought in the work of Charles Denby, author of *Indignant Heart: A Black Worker's Journal.* Denby, born in the South, became an auto worker in Detroit. Throughout his life, he rejected authoritarian control whether it came from the company, the union, or the left. He fought for grass-roots shop-floor organization with great courage and persistence. Aware of himself as a black worker in racist America, he recognized the importance of organizing workers in general and yet avoided the pitfalls of glamorizing "workers' power." Denby was especially alert to the dangers of Vanguard pretensions in leadership. When he heard the communist author Howard Fast argue that Paul Robeson was *the* leader who would take black people from bondage, he asked what would happen "if Robeson would pass on. All our hopes would be done."[33] For Denby, there could be no "Black Moses" to lead the people. The actions of resistance were too complex and too fluid to be guided by any one person or group. No one could draw up a blueprint for the future; it would have to be made and its shape determined by the actions of many. Reality was too complex for precise blueprints and marching orders:

> Few can look out upon a calm sea and tell when a storm will rise and the tides will sweep all filth to the shore. No one can set the time, date or place for the self activities of the Blacks as the Communist and other radical parties have tried to do.[34]

With all their plans and predictions, the leadership of parties and unions was often left behind by events created by the people.

> These so-called leaders were completely blind to what was happening. They simply could not believe that Blacks in the South, where the whole social, political, legal and economic system was organized to keep them in bondage, could succeed in fighting against such overwhelming force.[35]

Because the self-generated activities of people did not fit the plans, said Denby, groups ranging from the NAACP to the Communist Party and the unions were unprepared for the movement in the South and had to rush to catch up when they finally comprehended the significance of what was happening. The Montgomery bus boycott is a concrete example, for Denby, of the people surging ahead of the supposed leadership. As Denby says of the boycott that became the rallying point of the civil rights movement, "almost all the so-called leaders opposed it." The boycott emerged from the organizing and courage of people in Montgomery. "The boycott," said Denby, "was a result of a lot of things that had come together in Montgomery where Blacks have a history of doing things for themselves."[36]

Charles Denby's rejection of Vanguard claims of leadership and of precise blueprints for the future is not romantic speculation; it is based on his own activities and experiences. In his reliance on the indigenous political creativity of people, Denby testifies to the strength of Mutuality.

It is worth noting that Mutualistic tendencies are not confined to directly political manifestations like SNCC and SCLC. Mutuality can be found in important social and philosophical activities as well as in cultural work of writers and artists. Indeed, it is characteristic of black communities in general.

Examine, for a moment, both Ralph Ellison's commentary on the artist Romare Bearden and Bearden's own self-description.[37] Ellison points out that Bearden's work reflects the endurance and conscious creativity of everyday people. Bearden does not claim to be the voice of the people, as do some artists with more Vanguard aspirations. He does, Ellison says, bring the "eye of the painter, not that of the sociologist" to the depiction of Afro-American life. In this, he contributes a distinctive vision of places such as Harlem that reveals aspects of the people's existence that might not be seen through other methods. Ellison observes, "Through an act of creative will, he has blended strange visual harmonies out of the shrill, indigenous dichotomies of American life, and in so doing reflected the irrepressible thrust of a people to endure and keep its intimate sense of its own identity."[38]

Bearden says of himself that his task is to communicate in a fresh way that helps to illuminate realities not being adequately depicted through existing media. "What I've attempted to do is establish a world through art in which the validity of my Negro experience could live and make its own logic."[39] Bearden does not claim to be creating culture where there is none. Rather, through art, he seeks to communicate aspects of the existing culture. Bearden is engaging in that aspect of Mutuality that I have called the correspondence of communication. He takes part as a contributor rather than a leader. He is in accord with Ellison, who writes that "the role of the writer is that of a minor member, not the whole damned tribe." The artist, says Ellison, contributes "a small though necessary action."[40] The artist does not, in Ellison's view, seek to be the voice or the eyes of the people, but to draw from and transform what she or he finds in the world. "My goal," says Ellison, "is to work through, to transcend, as the blues transcend painful conditions with which they deal."[41] Again, we encounter the idea of transformation in the context of Mutuality. Ellison points out that transformation is not an intellectual act that only the *literati* and the *artistes* perform. Rather, such "working through" from the circumstances of life to the consciousness of life is what the people do: they do it in the blues, the music of the rural South and urban ghettos.

Neither Ellison nor Bearden claim to be simply one with the people; there is no such romanticism. Neither, however, do they imply that the creation of culture takes place only among the artists. Rather, as painter and writer, Bearden and Ellison create a particular kind of communication about life in America in a way that does not exist apart from their efforts. Once created, it becomes part of the mix, no more and no less than other contributions. Both Bearden and Ellison draw from the circumstances of black existences in America and do so in a Mutualistic way that communicates to the world at large. "I was trying," says Bearden, "to find out what was in me that was common to other men."[42]

Highly important examples of the tendency toward Mutuality among black writers can be found in the work of women authors and playwrights.[43] Writers such as Zora Neale Hurston, Lorraine Hansberry, Maya Angelou, Alice Walker, Ntoshake Shange, and Toni Cade Bambara describe in their work the commonplace yet extraordinary existence of average yet distinctive people fighting to be full human beings in a racist society. While their approaches are too diverse to reduce to one formula, we can note their common focus on Afro-American existence here in the United States. They honor the resilience and creative energy of people in their daily battle to build their lives. With their writers' eyes, they have added new dimensions of communication about Afro-American existence without romanticism but with a firm recognition of the activities of everyday lives. This communication of diverse forms of common struggle, the sensitivity to the indigenous creations of Afro-Americans, the expansiveness of the writing that reaches out to the world—all indicate the inclination toward Mutuality among these writers.

Music offers a number of interesting examples of Mutuality. The improvisational moment in Afro-American music or "jazz" is a vivid one. Notice what occurs. The musicians all bring their own particular instruments and approaches to the setting. They work within a given musical framework, a set of objective circumstances that derive from African and European antecedents as transformed in the furnace of the new world. They work within an agreed-upon musical setting. What they create is systematic; yet it is also highly unpredictable.

In contrast, the European classical symphony is eminently Vanguard in its form. Musicians work as an anonymous body to realize a plan set down in detail by a composer, directed and disciplined by a conductor. The orchestra marches along a well-marked road to a known destination. The improvisation of jazz is much more like those bands of people we met at the beginning of this book, hacking their individual paths through the forest. They call to one another with their instruments, encouraging each other and coordinating their efforts, until finally their paths meet joyously to create a common clearing.

Jazz musicians in their Mutuality are far from being anonymous. Those close to the music know who is on drums, what their story is, where they played last, and so on for everyone in the group. Unity and collaboration do not submerge the individual contributors.

Nor does musical praxis exhaust the examples of Mutuality in music. Take for example the Fort Apache Band of Jerry Gonzales, the great percussionist. Gonzalez describes the band members as "second generation [Afro-Hispanic-Indian] musicians living in N.Y.C."[44] Their music draws on their three cultural backgrounds and the metropolitan setting in which it is created. ("Fort Apache" was the nickname of a section of the Bronx.) As Enrique Fernandez points out, the:

> band, like its founding brothers (Andy and Jerry Gonzalez) is bilingual, the fusion comes from a deep understanding and command of Latin and jazz genres, and of the African tradition that precede them. . . . Theirs is music from an embattled territory, the barrio/ghetto, where the codes of third-world music meet and intermingle.[45]

The Fort Apache Band recognizes the corresponding circumstances that tie the music of composers such as Duke Ellington in North America to that of Chano Pozo in Latin

America. They attempt to communicate this correspondence through a music that consciously embodies that linkage. As Schomburg recognizes a variety of culinary traditions, they encompass a wide range of musics. The coming-together is made possible precisely because the elements are so diverse and distinctive. It is their distinctiveness grounded in commonality that makes their record, "The River Is Deep," an example of the Mutualistic approach. In their version of Bud Powell's *Parisian Thoroughfare*, the jazz classic is set "to the powerful rhythms of *guaguanco*, the Cuban street rhythm," and Dizzy Gillespie's *Bebop* is set to Afro-Cuban "*comparza* rhythms."[46] The record opens with a chant to the West African Yoruba deity Elegua and the closing number is "Wawina Era Wo," a chant for another Yoruba deity using a *cuatro*, the traditional Puerto Rican guitar as part of the instrumentation.

Africa is an important source of the band's music, but it is not a distant mythical Africa. Rather, it is the living transformed Africa, as maintained and developed by people in such diverse areas as Puerto Rico, Cuba, New York, and elsewhere. The chant to the Yoruba deity is actually a traditional Cuban song. Its performance by musicians living in New York is not a folkloric preservation. Rather, it maintains a living tradition. At the same time, through its fusion with black American music, the song is a new creation. Thus, existing forms are respected, utilized, and transformed, becoming new form that is as much a "reflection of our experience here in New York" as it is of Africa or Cuba or Puerto Rico.[47]

This is an expansive endeavor. It does not remain locked in one static cultural preserve. It does not seek to maintain a pristine past. Neither does it denigrate the past or the products of everyday people. It draws from them and transforms them and in so doing becomes part of the very living traditions that it reflects and transforms. Interestingly, that "embattled territory," the "barrio/ghetto" whose musicians ride and channel the cross-circulating currents of many cultures, is very close to Schomburg's description of "rattlesnakes under the El" where living aspects of black culture around the world come together in Harlem. This simultaniety is not just accidental. Like Schomburg, the Fort

Apache Band, in its respect for and utilization of indigenous cultural forms, in its recognition of existing corresponding circumstances, and in its push to communicate those circumstances, is deeply Mutualistic in its actions.

One final political-musical example of Mutuality is found in the work of the socialist humanist, C. L. R. James. In 1961, James wrote an essay on the famous calypso singer known as the Mighty Sparrow. He described how the Mighty Sparrow, a man from and of the working people, has developed an astute political analysis of the Caribbean in his music. The Mighty Sparrow is not college educated, nor is he a formally trained singer. Yet, for James and for millions in the Caribbean, the Mighty Sparrow communicates information and analysis. He is able to do this, says James, because "his talents were shaped by a West Indian medium" and it is "through this medium that he expands his capacities and the medium itself." Because his music is grounded in everyday life and culture, it is immediately accessible to a broad range of people. The Mighty Sparrow employs this cultural dimension to develop his own work, to expand and disseminate it. His is no static imitation of existing tradition. He also transforms the music by expanding the medium itself, as James says.[48]

I see important Mutualistic features in this. There is the actual correspondence of circumstances, the West Indian medium within which he makes his music. There is also the communication of these circumstances via the medium of the music itself. Moreover, the circumstances are not just depicted; they are challenged and transformed in the act of communication.

James says of the Mighty Sparrow, "What attracts and holds me is his social and political sense, and his independence and fearlessness. Most important, the Mighty Sparrow is a deliberate originator of his own political analysis. Consequently, he cannot be seen as a mere reaction to political stimulus. He can, and must, be viewed with respect as an active person seeking to transform his world. He will, says James, find "his own way, using whatever is done, ignoring it or denouncing it as he pleases," whatever the intellectuals may or may not say about him.[49]

Note what James does in this essay. He recognizes his

own intellectual and political kinship with the Mighty Sparrow, and he proclaims that he and the Sparrow are engaged in the same battles. James uses the pen, the Mighty Sparrow uses music; they are distinctly different, yet linked in their striving for justice and in their attempt to communicate that battle. They are linked in their respect for peoples' capacity to understand complex issues and they aim to illuminate that capacity. In recognizing the Mighty Sparrow as a fellow pilgrim, one using a different means of locomotion, James places himself on the same plane. His analysis does not place him on the Vanguard high seat. James himself is an example of Mutualistic action.

James's tendencies toward Mutuality trace in part to a major Marxist revolt against Stalinism. This revolt emphasized the capacity of people to run society without the heavy-handed direction of centralized bureaucratic elites. Yet, just as the Vanguard tendency in the work of people such as George Jackson and the Black Panther Party cannot simply be traced to Marxism but must be understood within the environment of black American social thought, so too must James's Marxist Mutuality be placed in context. Once again we find an interesting example of European and Third World Marxist tendencies paralleling or intersecting with Afro-American political thought. It is clear that in both its Vanguard and Mutualistic tendencies, black American social thought is often paralleled by similar currents in Europe. Yet we have seen how this thought cannot be reduced to concepts such as conservative and radical. Rather, black American social thought has its own distinctive indigenous features. Nevertheless, the intriguing parallels between different situations indicate that how to organize effectively while also maintaining egalitarian cooperative social modes has been and continues to be a basic problem around the world.

Future Possibilities

In the 1980's, the Rev. Jesse Jackson and his supporters, brought together the Rainbow Coalition. Many media stories focused on Jackson and his charisma, ignoring the grass-roots aspects of the Rainbow Coalition. Nonetheless, in many areas the coalition emerged from local actions. For example, in Western Massachusetts those involved, as the coalition's name implies, included blacks, whites, Hispanics, unionists, environmentalists, and college students. But the inevitable media attention on the leader, and the lack of coverage of local grass-roots aspects, were in some ways abetted by the coalition itself. The Rainbow Coalition, to a large extent, remained locked in the embrace of Jesse Jackson as "the leader" even as many thousands of everyday people were making the entire effort possible. Thus the movement continued to demonstrate the basic weakness of *de facto* Mutuality that is not recognized or celebrated. When Mutuality remains underground, the more Vanguard perspective tendencies in the wider society are left as the most prominent framework for viewing and analyzing social movements. The habits of the media and the attractions of leadership will conspire to ignore Mutualistic efforts even when they are occurring in full force. This is why effective instances of Mutuality, both historically and in the present, must be made apparent. Those who called for the "institutionalization" of the Rainbow Coalition, so that it would have an existence apart from Jesse Jackson, did indeed see the need for making the grass-roots realities more visible and organizationally sound. Certainly a movement would be much more resiliant if it were not dependent on one person and if it involved the conscious participation of many people. Such participation gives people a concrete sense that they can make things happen. This knowledge, once gained, cannot be taken away, no matter what happens to the leaders.

As this book was being written, Rainbow Coalition activities suggested that indeed a more overt Mutualistic focus was being worked out. In the 1986 organizing convention of the Coalition, representatives from the North American Farmers Alliance joined with black inner-city organizers, environmentalists, Free South Africa activists, Latinos, and trade unionists, among others. The attempt by Jesse Jackson to reach out through the coalition to groups that previously had had no contact, even at the personal level, with black people, had at this point been quite successful. Roger Allison, executive director of the Missouri Rural Crisis Center, observed that the thousands of farmers addressed by Jackson in Missouri in 1986 "had never seen a black person before, and if they had seen a black person before they certainly hadn't seen one who could stand up and articulate our issues better than we could."[50] (Indeed, Jackson and the Rainbow Coalition were the only forces addressing farmers' issues outside of farm groups themselves.)

The 1986 convention represented a conscious effort by Jackson and others to create an ongoing organization that would not be totally dependent on Jackson. To the degree that this can be accomplished, and to the degree that the Rainbow Coalition continues to reach out to groups not previously included in black-white alliances, then a more overt Mutualistic approach is a real possibility. It is important to note that Jackson himself has played a major role in promoting the "institutionalization" effort that would remove some of the excessive emphasis on him personally.

The Rainbow Coalition is the first black-initiated national political action that white people have joined, not because they felt they had to help black people but because the coalition is one major force addressing particular issues such as the environment, nuclear war, and farm crises. It is a further mark of the success of the Rainbow Coalition that it is maintaining its black dimension while reaching out to other groups to further their own objectives.

For the moment, the Rainbow Coalition is an important nationwide embodiment of Mutualistic tendencies. It draws in diverse groups without requiring that those groups give up their particular concerns in favor of one blueprint and one leader. The Rainbow Coalition addresses a wide range of social-political domains, including U.S. foreign policy, the environment, the farm crisis, and black-white equality. The greatest weakness of the Rainbow Coalition is one that runs through earlier Mutualistic efforts. It has not overcome the tendency to focus, both within and outside the movement, on one person, and to marginalize the significant efforts of many people. But this dilemma indicates the importance of bringing Mutuality to light as a cohesive world view so that it will be less subject to the corrosive emphasis on elite leadership.

Like the UNIA, the Rainbow Coalition has not confined its Mutualistic message to the United States. The coalition has established strong ties to various anti-apartheid movements in South Africa. In particular, links with the United Democratic Front (UDF) have been made. The United Democratic Front, in turn, is itself a vast coalition of township organizers, church groups, trade unionists, students, and others. In its turn, the UDF has a close working relationship with the huge Congress of South African Trade Unions (COSATU). Both vast movements have also expressed support for the African National Congress.

It is characteristic of the difficulty of attempting to analyze Mutualistic action through categories such as East versus West that the black trade unionists support the African National Congress, which has a historic working relationship with the South African Communist Party among many other groups, while those same unionists also strongly support the Solidarity movement in Poland. COSATU views Solidarity's struggle for worker control as parallel to their own. If we pursue this fluid intersection of various movements further, we can see that Solidarity is also supported by the various Green movements in Western Europe. Thus the Rainbow Coalition is tied to a variety of coalitions in South Africa which in turn have reached out to Solidarity in Poland. The "Polish connection" links these groups to the Greens in Europe—as does the Rainbow Coalition's agenda on environmental issues. There is no end to the globe-circling connections.

All of this correspondence between groups, from the United States to South Africa to Poland and back, suggests a vast Mutualistic tendency that cuts across national boundaries and goes against the dominant discourse of East-West conflict. Moreover, in characteristic Mutualistic fashion, there is in this network no one overarching schema or leader. Instead the picture is highly fluid, complex, and difficult to confine in traditional categories. While these are globe-circling movements, they grow from diverse local grass-roots organizations in township, ghetto, farmhouse, factory, and church. They are simultaneously vast and highly intimate and personal, movements that speak and listen to the person as well as to the people. Consequently, knowledge of what is happening to local activists in one part of the world has the potential of being shared with those in another part of the world. Such sharing of information is not complete, of course, but the globe-circling channels of communication among Mutualistically inclined movements open many possibilities. This is not mass communication with information being dispensed from one global center. Rather it is a potentially expanding and deepening network of shared information among a huge variety of local areas, one that infiltrates national and ideological barriers. Mutuality is a promise and a living reality in today's world.

The Vanguard perspective and Mutuality exist as fundamental world views within key areas of black American social thought. Their operation and significance, however, is obscured by the more traditional debates that talk of conservatism versus radicalism or Marxism versus nationalism. The Vanguard Perspective exerts tremendous influence on general thinking precisely because it is not recognized as the coherent systematic approach that it is. Instead, it appears simply as a natural way of looking at social action. Leaders and leading groups, with their special knowledge and blueprints for action, are seen just as a basic human way of being political. In truth, the Vanguard perspective is a world view, born in reaction to particular circumstances, real and imagined, that attempts to enhance the privileged position of particular elites. It is a social, political, and philosophic phenomenon. It must be recognized as such.

Mutuality, by contrast, suffers from obscurity. Lacking heros and banners, it works unnoticed although it is essential to human enterprise. So powerful are the cultural tendencies to think in power-centered and competitive terms that Mutualistic action is often profoundly undervalued by the very people who employ it. We must recognize and honor Mutuality so that the creative power of local people is not overlooked and neglected. Without the efforts of those who work locally and think globally, few profound changes can be achieved.

It is my hope that we will act to strengthen mutuality, that we will remember that what is created by people can be changed by people.

Notes

Preface

1. Clifford Geertz, *The Interpretation of Cultures* (New York: Basic Books, 1973), p. 127.

Chapter 1

1. Giordano Bruno, *On The Infinite*, trans. John Toland (London: J. Peale, 1726). For a discussion of Bruno, see Arthur Lovejoy, *The Great Chain of Being: A Study in the History of an Idea* (Cambridge: Harvard Univ. Press, 1936).

2. Malcolm X, "You're Going to Catch Hell Just Like Me," on *Malcolm X: By Any Means Necessary* (New York: Douglass Communications, stereo recording no. Z-30743).

3. Antonio Gramsci, *Selections from Political Writings: 1910–1920* (New York: International Publishers, 1977), p. 131.

4. "Interview with Ella Jo Baker and Fannie Lou Hamer," *Southern Exposure* 1 (1981): 47.

Chapter 2

1. W. E. B. Du Bois, *The Philadelphia Negro, A Social Study* (New York: Shocken Books, 1967), p. 97. For a perspective on Du Bois and Booker T. Washington different from the analysis developed in my work, see Louis R. Harlan, *Booker T. Washington, The Making of a Black Leader 1856–1911* (Oxford: Oxford Univ. Press, 1972); and August Meier, *Negro Thought in America, 1880–1915, Racial Ideologies in the Age of Booker T. Washington* (Ann Arbor: Univ. of Michigan Press, 1973).

2. Du Bois, *Philadelphia Negro*, pp. 97–98.

150 NOTES FOR CHAPTER 2

3. See, for example, John Hope Franklin, *From Slavery to Freedom: A History of Negro Americans* (New York: Knopf, 1969); John Blassingame, *The Slave Community: Plantation Life in the Ante-Bellum South* (Oxford: Oxford Univ. Press, 1980); Albert Raboteau, *Slave Religion: The Invisible Institution in the Antebellum South* (New York: Oxford Univ. Press, 1980); and Peter Rachleff, *Black Labor in the South: Richmond, Virginia 1865–1896* (Philadelphia: Temple Univ. Press, 1984).

4. For a discussion of the Makno populist movement, see Paul Avrich, *The Russian Anarchists* (New York: Norton, 1978). Also important for discussion of grass-roots action is Jeremy Brecher's *Strike!* (Boston: South End Press, 1977).

5. Booker T. Washington, *The Booker T. Washington Papers*, 13 vols., ed. Louis R. Harlan, Stuart B. Kaufman, and Raymond W. Smock (Chicago: Univ. of Illinois Press, 1972–1984), 3:505.

6. Ibid., 5:345.

7. Ibid.

8. Washington, *The Story of the Negro: The Rise of the Race from Slavery* (New York: Doubleday, 1909), 2:71.

9. Ibid.

10. Washington, *Papers*, 4:373.

11. Washington, *The Selected Speeches of Booker T. Washington*, ed. E. E. Washington (Garden City, N.Y.: Doubleday, 1932), p. 255.

12. W. E. B. Du Bois, *The Souls of Black Folk* (Greenwich, Conn.: Fawcett Publications, 1961), p. 140.

13. Ibid., p. 141.

14. Ibid., p. 19.

15. Ibid., p. 87.

16. Ibid., p. 51.

17. Ibid., p. 73.

18. Washington, *Papers*, 7:95.

19. Ibid., 2:271. Washington's emphasis on the power of money led him to *support the idea of boycotts against public transportation as a means of exerting influence.* He wrote, "No street railway in the South will pay [make profit] if Negro patronage is withdrawn." Washington, *Papers*, 3:410.

20. Karl Marx and Frederick Engels, *The Communist Manifesto* (Baltimore: Penguin Books, 1967), p. 82. In his 1910 trip to Europe, Washington met with socialists. He was familiar with what he called their "doctrines," and praised the Socialist Party of Sicily. See Washington, *The Man Furthest Down: A Record of Observation and Study in Europe* (New York: Doubleday, Page and Co., 1912).

21. Washington, *Papers*, 3:410.
22. Ibid.
23. Ibid., p. 478.
24. Ibid., 4:139.
25. Ibid., 3:478.
26. Ibid., 5:339.
27. Ibid., 3:437.
28. Ibid., p. 111.
29. Ibid., 4:373.
30. Washington, "Industrial Education for the Negro," in *The Negro Problem* (New York: Arno Press and the *New York Times*, 1969), pp. 15–16. This is a consistent theme in Washington's thought. For a similar version, see Washington, *Up From Slavery: An Autobiography* (New York: Bantam Books, 1967), ch. 5.
31. Washington, *Papers*, 3:185.
32. Ibid., p. 186.
33. Ibid., p. 200.
34. Ibid., 4:370.
35. Ibid., 7:235.
36. Washington, *Selected Speeches*, p. 226.
37. Ibid.
38. Washington, *Papers*, 3:22.
39. Du Bois, "World War and the Color Line," *The Crisis* 9 (1914): 28–30.
40. Du Bois, *W. E. B. Du Bois Speaks: Speeches and Addresses 1890–1920*, ed. Philip S. Foner (New York: Pathfinder, 1970), p. 251.
41. Ibid., pp. 251–52.
42. Ibid., p. 252.
43. Ibid., p. 255.
44. Ibid.
45. Du Bois, *Darkwater: Voices from within the Veil* (New York: Harcourt, Brace, and Co., 1921), p. 39.
46. Du Bois, "Negro Education," *The Crisis* 15 (1918): 175.
47. Du Bois, *Darkwater*, p. 158.
48. Ibid., pp. 158–59.
49. Du Bois, "Josiah Royce," *The Crisis* 13 (1916): 10–11.
50. Du Bois, "Tagore," *The Crisis* 13 (1916): 60–61.
51. Du Bois, *Du Bois Speaks*, p. 116.
52. Ibid.
53. Du Bois, "The Shadow of the Years," *The Crisis* 15 (1918): 170.
54. Du Bois, *Du Bois Speaks*, p. 91.
55. Du Bois, *Darkwater*, p. 159.

56. Ibid.
57. Du Bois, as editor, reprinted John Ruskin's interpretation of Turner's painting, "The Slaveship," in *The Crisis* 15 (1918): 239.
58. Du Bois, *Souls*, p. 22.
59. Du Bois, *The Negro* (Oxford: Oxford Univ. Press, 1970), p. 22.
60. Ibid., p. 23.
61. Du Bois, *Du Bois Speaks*, p. 198.
62. Du Bois, *Souls*, p. 87.
63. Ibid., p. 21.
64. Ibid., p. 86.
65. Ibid., p. 72.
66. Ibid., p. 19.
67. Ibid.
68. Du Bois, *Darkwater*, p. 29.

Chapter 3

1. "The Socialist Expulsion," *The Messenger*, Dec. 1919, p. 2. For discussion of *The Messenger*, see, Jervis Anderson, *A. Philip Randolph: A Biographical Portrait* (New York: Harcourt Brace Jovanovich, 1973), and Harold Cruse, *Crisis of the Negro Intellectual* (New York: William Morrow, 1967).
2. "The Socialist Expulsion," Dec. 1919, p. 2.
3. "Should Negroes be Socialists?" *Messenger*, Oct. 1920, p. 106.
4. A. Philip Randolph, "A New Crowd, A New Negro," *Messenger*, May-June 1919, p. 26.
5. A. Philip Randolph, "When the War Will End." *Messenger*, Aug. 1919, pp. 16–17.
6. Ibid.
7. Ibid., pp. 18, 20.
8. Ibid., p. 20.
9. W. A. Domingo, "Private Property as a Pillar of Prejudice," *Messenger*, Aug. 1920, p. 71.
10. Ibid.
11. "The Causes and Remedy of Race Riots," *Messenger*, Sept. 1919, p. 13.
12. A. Philip Randolph, "When the War Will End," *Messenger*, Aug. 1919, p. 20.
13. "The Russian Triumph," *Messenger*, March 1920, pp. 3–4.
14. W. A. Domingo, "Did Bolshevism Stop Race Riots in Russia?" *Messenger*, Sept. 1919, p. 26.
15. Ibid.
16. Ibid., and "Get Out of Russia," *Messenger*, March 1919, p. 7.

17. Randolph, "A New Crowd, A New Negro," p. 26.
18. "The International Debacle," *Messenger*, Nov. 1920, p. 135.
19. W. A. Domingo, "A New Negro and a New Day," *Messenger*, Nov. 1920, p. 144.
20. Ibid.
21. Ibid.
22. "Africa for the Africans," *Messenger*, Sept. 1920, p. 84.
23. "The New Negro—What is He?" *Messenger*, Aug. 1920, p. 74.
24. Ibid.
25. Florette Henri, *Black Migration: Movement North 1900–1920, The Road from Myth to Man* (Garden City, N.Y.: Doubleday, 1976), p. 267.
26. William N. Colson, "An Analysis of Negro Patriotism," *Messenger*, Aug. 1919, p. 24.
27. "Chicago Rebellion, Free Black Men Fight Free White Men," *Messenger*, Sept. 1919, p. 30.
28. Ibid., p. 32.
29. Ibid., pp. 31–32.
30. "The Negro, a Menace to Radicalism?" *Messenger*, May-June 1919, p. 20.
31. Ibid.
32. "The Negro Radicals," *Messenger*, Sept. 1919, p. 18.
33. "Organizing the Negro Actor," *Messenger*, July 1919, p. 12.
34. "Strikes," *Messenger*, Sept. 1919, pp. 6–7.
35. "The New Philosophy of the Negro," *Messenger*, Dec. 1919, p. 5.
36. Lovett Fort-Whiteman, "The Lincoln Theater," *Messenger*, Nov. 1917, p. 29.
37. Fort-Whiteman, "On Tragedy," *Messenger*, Nov. 1917, p. 30.
38. Fort-Whiteman, "Naturalism in Literature," *Messenger*, Nov. 1918, p. 25.
39. "W. E. B. Du Bois," *Messenger*, July 1918, pp. 27–28.
40. Chandler Owen, "The Failure of Negro Leaders," *Messenger*, Nov. 1918, p. 24.
41. William Colson, "Phases of Du Bois," *Messenger*, April-May 1920, p. 11.
42. George Frazier Miller, "The Social Value of the Uncultured," *Messenger*, Sept. 1919, p. 31.
43. See n. 38, ch. 2.
44. Miller, "The Social Value of the Uncultured," p. 31.
45. Robert Hayden, Introduction to *The New Negro*, ed. Alain Locke (New York: Atheneum, 1977), p. ix. For discussions of the Harlem Renaissance and the concept of the "New Negro," see Nathan Huggins, *Harlem Renaissance* (New York: Oxford Univ.

Press, 1974), and Harold Cruse, *The Crisis of the Negro Intellectual* (New York: William Morrow, 1967).

46. Herskovits's later scholarly interest in African retentions in the Americas was a development that clearly followed in the wake of black writers like Arthur Huff Fauset and W. E. B. Du Bois. Both of those writers had already posited some survival of African culture in North America. A study of the relationship between these earlier perspectives, and the later work of Herskovits, is needed.

47. Melville Herskovits, "The Negro's Americanism," in *The New Negro*, pp. 354, 358–59, 360.

48. Ibid., pp. 359, 353.

49. Ibid., p. 359.

50. James Weldon Johnson, "Harlem: the Cultural Capital," *New Negro*, pp. 301, 309.

51. Ibid., pp. 309–10.

52. Ibid., p. 311.

53. J. W. Johnson, "Harlem, Cultural Capital," p. 301.

54. Ibid., p. 309.

55. Ibid.

56. Charles S. Johnson, "The New Frontage on American Life," *New Negro*, p. 285.

57. Ibid., p. 286.

58. Charles Johnson's views were consistent with the Chicago school of sociology at the University of Chicago, where he completed his education.

59. C. Johnson, "The New Frontage," p. 287.

60. Arthur Huff Fauset, "American Negro Folk Literature," *New Negro*, p. 243.

61. Ibid., p. 241.

62. Alain Locke, "The New Negro," *New Negro*, p. 4.

63. Ibid., p. 7.

64. Alain Locke, "The Negro Spirituals," *New Negro*, p. 200.

65. Alain Locke, "Negro Youth Speaks," *New Negro*, p. 51.

66. Alain Locke, "The Legacy of the Ancestral Arts," *New Negro*, p. 267.

67. Ibid., p. 294.

68. Charles S. Johnson, "The New Frontage on American Life," p. 297.

69. Locke, "The New Negro," p. 7.

70. Ibid., p. 15.

71. Locke, "The Negro Spirituals," p. 200.

72. Ibid.

73. Ibid., p. 205.
74. Locke, "The New Negro," p. 9.
75. Locke, "The Negro Spirituals," p. 207.
76. A. H. Fauset, "American Negro Folk Literature," *New Negro*, p. 243.
77. Locke, "The Legacy of the Ancestral Arts," p. 255.
78. Henry Louis Gates, personal communication, 1979.

Chapter 4

1. W. E. B. Du Bois, "G. W. Ellis, *Negro Culture in West Africa*," *The Crisis* 2 (1915): 200. See also George W. Ellis, *Negro Culture in West Africa* (New York: Neale Publishing, 1914).
2. St. Clair Drake, "Anthropology and the Black Experience," *The Black Scholar, Journal of Black Studies and Research* (September/October 1980): 2.
3. Rayford Logan and Michael Winston, "George Washington Ellis," in *The Dictionary of American Negro Biography* (New York: W.W. Norton, 1982), p. 212. J. A. Rogers in his syndicated column called Ellis, "one of the leading authorities on African life and manners of his time." Chicago *Daily News*, 13 Nov. 1914. The article, "Says Islam is Ready to Join in the War," described Ellis as a man "whose fingers, it is asserted, rest on the great black pulse of Africa." This article can be found in the G. W. Ellis Papers at the Chicago Historical Society. For an important discussion of Ellis's work, see John E. Fleming, "George Washington Ellis and Africa, 1902–1910" (M.A. Thesis, Howard University, 1972).
4. See Logan and Winston, "Ellis," p. 212.
5. George W. Ellis, "The Psychology of American Race Prejudice," *Journal of Race Development* 3 (1915): 300–301.
6. Ibid., p. 303.
7. Ibid.
8. Ibid., pp. 303–4.
9. Ibid., p. 304.
10. George W. Ellis, "Psychic Factors in the New American Race Situation," *Journal of Race Development* 4 (1917): 485.
11. Ibid.
12. Ibid., p. 486.
13. Ellis, "The Psychology of American Race Prejudice," p. 312.
14. Ellis, "Psychic Factors," p. 486.
15. Ibid., p. 486.
16. Ibid., pp. 468, 469.

17. Ibid.
18. Harold Barron, "The Demand for Black Labor: Historical Notes on the Political Economy of Racism," *Radical America* 2 (1971): 16–17.
19. Ibid.
20. Ellis, "Psychic Factors," p. 469.
21. George W. Ellis, "The Negro in the War for Democracy," *Journal of Race Development* 4 (1918): 442, 443.
22. George W. Ellis, "Reform and the Negro in Chicago," *The Boston Citizen* (no. 1, 1915), p. 10.
23. Ibid., p. 11.
24. Ellis, "Psychology of American Race Prejudice," p. 297.
25. There has been much dispute whether dialect is folk language or racist caricature. For discussion of this issue, see Sterling Brown, *Negro Poetry and Drama and the Negro in American Fiction* (New York: Atheneum, 1978), and Henry Louis Gates, "Dis and Dat: Dialect and Descent," in *Afro-American Literature, the Reconstruction of an Institution* (New York: Modern Language Association of America, 1979).
26. George W. Ellis, "The Mission of Dunbar," *The Boston Citizen* (no. 2, 1915), p. 63.
27. Ibid., p. 61.
28. Ibid., p. 63.
29. See Gates, "Dis and Dat."
30. Ellis, "Mission of Dunbar," p. 67.
31. Ivan Turgenev, *Smoke* (New York: Boni and Liveright, 1919), p. 36.
32. Concomitantly, Schomburg felt that through rigorous scholarly investigation, materials on black people could be, and were being found. For example, see his "Sebastian Gomez," in *The Crisis* 11 (1916): 136–137. (Note that Schomburg often Anglicized his first name, Arturo.)
33. Arthur Schomburg, *Racial Integrity: A Plea for the Establishment of a Chair of Negro History in Our Schools and Colleges, Etc.* (Yonkers, New York: Negro Society for Historical Research [Occasional Paper no. 3], 1913), p. 1.
34. Juan Latino was an African-Spanish writer in the sixteenth century. Born a slave, he was given the chair of poetry at the University of Grenada and was acclaimed "the most learned in the Latin language," writes Schomburg in *Racial Integrity*, p. 8. This was the type of historical information that Schomburg declared had been systematically suppressed as part of the oppression of black people. Schomburg believed that Carter Woodson's Negro

Society for Historical Research was playing a vital role in pursuing such research. For discussion of Woodson, see John Hope Franklin, "The New Negro History," *Journal of Negro History* (no. 2, 1957), pp. 89–97.

35. William Ferris, *The African Abroad*, 2 vols. (New Haven: Tuttle, Morehouse, and Taylor Press, 1913); Benjamin Brawley, *A Social History of the American Negro* (New York: MacMillan, 1921).

36. Arthur Schomburg, Notes on "Africa Free States," Schomburg Papers, Box 11, in the New York Public Library's Schomburg Center for Research in Black Culture.

37. Ibid.

38. Schomburg, *Racial Integrity*, pp. 5–6.

39. Schomburg, "The Negro Digs Up His Past," in *The New Negro*, p. 231. Although included in *The New Negro*, Schomburg's article, viewed in the larger context of his writing, moved in a quite different direction from Locke's work.

40. Ibid., pp. 231–32.

41. Schomburg, *Racial Integrity*, p. 12.

42. Schomburg, "The Negro Digs," p. 236.

43. Ibid., p. 237.

44. Schomburg, *Racial Integrity*, pp. 14, 6.

45. Schomburg, "The Negro Digs," p. 232.

46. Schomburg, *Racial Integrity*, p. 19.

47. Schomburg, Proposal for a Book on Afro-American Culinary Arts and Culture, typescript (undated, untitled. I estimate that it was written in the early 1920s). This document can be found in the Schomburg Papers, Box 12, in the New York Public Library's Schomburg Center for Research in Black Culture.

48. Ibid., p. 1.

49. Ibid., pp. 3, 3, 6.

50. Ibid., pp. 4–5.

51. Ibid., p. 9.

52. Ibid., p. 6.

53. Ibid., p. 9.

54. Ibid.

55. Ibid., p. 8.

56. Ibid. The reasons for the reservations about pork are not evident.

57. Ibid., p. 7.

58. Ibid., pp. 7, 10.

59. Ibid., p. 8.

60. Ibid., p. 1.

61. Ibid., p. 6.

62. See for example, Franz Boas, "The Methods of Ethnology," *American Anthropologist* (no. 26, 1920). Boas was a progressive on race compared to his contemporaries, but he sought to extract the form of American Indian culture from what he saw as a "dying" people and so paralleled *The New Negro* emphasis on the search for artifactual, rather than living, culture. For an important example of the transformational power of living Afro-American culture, listen to Zydeco music from Louisiana. Zydeco is a conscious Afro-American fusion of French Acadian and African rhythms of urban and rural blues, and of Caribbean and North American musical forms. Listen to Clifton Chenier on *Classic Clifton* (El Cerrito, Calif.: Arhoolie Records, no. Ar-19045), and *Les Blues Du Bayou* (Washington, D.C.: Spottswood Music, no. MLP 7330). For a discussion of this area, see Jim and Carolotta Anderson, "The Good Times are Rolling in Cajun Country," *Smithsonian* 18 (1988): 112–27.

63. Schomburg, Proposal, p. 9.

64. Ibid., p. 10.

65. W. Wilson, "Gimmie a Pigfoot," (originally on Okeh Records, no. 8949). A release of this song, as sung by Bessie Smith, can be found on *Bessie Smith, the World's Greatest Blues Singer* (New York: Columbia Records, no. GP 33).

66. For a useful discussion of Frazier and classic urban sociology see G. Franklin Edwards, "E. Franklin Frazier," in *Black Sociologists, Historical and Contemporary Perspectives*, ed. James E. Blackwell and Morris Janowitz (Chicago: Univ. of Chicago, 1974), pp. 85–120.

67. These implications of Schomburg's proposal are an important foreshadowing of arguments by Amilcar Cabral, secretary-general of the African Party for the Independence of Guinea and the Cape Verde Islands, who was assassinated by Portuguese agents in 1973. Cabral wrote that, under oppression, African "culture took refuge in the villages" and "in the spirit of the victims of domination." Consequently, there could be no "question of a 'return to the source,' or of a 'cultural renaissance.'" Unlike the intellectual elites who had turned away from their culture, the everyday folk of the villages were "the only social sector who can preserve and build it up and make history." Cabral, *Return to the Source: Selected Speeches of Amilcar Cabral*, edited by the African Information Service (New York: The Monthly Review Press, 1973), p. 61.

68. Tony Martin, *Race First: The Ideological and Organizational Struggles of Marcus Garvey and the Universal Negro Improve-*

ment Association (Westport, Conn.: Greenwood Press, 1976), is required reading on this subject. For an important earlier work, see J. A. Cronon, *Black Moses: The Story of Marcus Garvey and the Universal Negro Improvement Association* (Madison: Univ. of Wisconsin Press, 1969). *The Marcus Garvey and Universal Negro Improvement Association Papers*, ed. Robert A. Hill et al., 5 vols. to date (Berkeley and Los Angeles: Univ. of California Press, 1983), is invaluable. The literature on Marcus Garvey and the Universal Negro Improvement Association is extensive. For a useful bibliography see *Marcus Garvey, Life and Lessons*, ed. Robert A. Hill and Barbara Blair (Berkeley and Los Angeles: Univ. of California Press, 1987).

69. Marcus Garvey, *Philosophy and Opinions of Marcus Garvey*, ed. Amy Jacques Garvey, 3 vols. (New York: Atheneum, 1974), 2:111, 37, 97.

70. Ibid., p. 15.

71. Ibid., p. 79.

72. Tony Martin, *Race First* (quoting from a UNIA correspondent in *Negro World*), pp. 92–93. See also the *Garvey Papers*, 4:745.

73. Garvey, *Philosophy*, 2:15.

74. Ibid., 1:9.

75. Garvey, *Papers*, 4:1019.

76. Ibid., p. 764.

77. Garvey, *Philosophy*, 2:19, and *Papers*, 4:1019. The UNIA's Committee on the Future of the Negro in America, meeting in 1922, called for a "chair of Negro history," echoing Schomburg's 1913 statement, "Racial Integrity, Plea for the Establishment of a Chair of Negro History."

78. Garvey, *Philosophy*, 2:19.

79. Ibid., p. 71, and *Papers*, 4:175.

80. See *Marcus Garvey and the Vision of Africa*, ed. John Henrick Clarke, with Amy Jacques Garvey (New York: Random House, 1974), p. 192.

81. C. L. R. James, *The Future in the Present* (Westport, Conn.: Lawrence Hill, 1977), p. 209. Also see J. H. Clarke in *Marcus Garvey and the Vision of Africa*, p. 197.

82. Ted Vincent, "The Harlem to Bluefields Connection, Sandino's Aid from the Black American Press," *The Black Scholar* (May/June 1985): 36. For an important contemporary development of certain key themes raised by Schomburg and Garvey, see Molefi Kete Asante, *The Afrocentric Idea* (Philadelphia: Temple University Press, 1987).

Chapter 5

1. Elijah Muhammad, *Message to the Blackman in America* (Chicago: Muhammad Mosque of Islam No. 2, 1965), pp. 65, 70.
2. Ibid., p. 169.
3. Cited in C. Eric Lincoln, *The Black Muslims in America* (Boston: Beacon Press, 1961), pp. 69–70.
4. Ibid., p. 89.
5. Ibid., p. 91.
6. E. Muhammad, *Message*, p. 65.
7. Ibid., p. 287.
8. For example, see, "Haiti, the Storm and Stagnation," *Muhammad Speaks*, September 1970, p. 15, for commentary on Vodun as "superstition." In taking this position, the Nation entered a basic African conflict. For continental African discussion of the relationship between Islam, Christianity, and the indigenous African religions see Abdullahi Smith, "The Early States of the Central Sudan," in *History of West Africa*, 2 vols., ed. J. F. A. Ajayi and Michael Crowder (New York: Columbia Univ. Press, 1972), pp. 158–201; and Lamin O. Sanneh, *West African Christianity: The Religious Impact* (Cambridge: Cambridge Univ. Press, 1983).
9. C. L. R. James, *The Black Jacobins: Toussaint L'Overture and the San Domingo Revolution* (New York: Vintage Books, 1963), p. 394.
10. George Jackson, *Soledad Brother: The Prison Letters of George Jackson* (New York: Bantam, 1970), pp. 131–32. For an example of Black Panther Party vanguard philosophy, see "An Interview with Huey P. Newton," in *Black Nationalism in America*, ed. John H. Bracey et al. (Indianapolis: Bobbs-Merrill, 1970), pp. 534–51.
11. Ibid., p. 91.
12. Ibid., p. 133.
13. Ibid., p. 91.
14. Ibid., pp. 99, 131, 123, 88.
15. Harold Cruse, *The Crisis of the Negro Intellectual*, pp. 542, 472.
16. Ibid., pp. 455, 457, 475.
17. Ibid., p. 451.
18. Hardy T. Frye, *Black Parties and Political Power: A Case Study* (Boston: G.K. Hall, 1980), p. 46. This is an important analysis of the civil rights struggle and of third-party organizing efforts. For analysis of "cosmopolitans," and "locals," see Joyce Ladner, "What Black Power Means to Negroes in Mississippi," in

Black Liberation Politics: A Reader, ed. Edward Greer (Boston: Allyn and Bacon, 1971). The indomitable Ella Baker played a key role in encouraging the Mutualistic tendencies of SNCC.

19. Frye, *Black Parties*, pp. 45, 47.

20. Ibid., p. 48.

21. Ibid., pp. 48–49.

22. Ibid., pp. 49, 52.

23. Stokely Carmichael and Charles V. Hamilton, *Black Power: The Politics of Liberation in America* (New York: Vintage Books, 1967), p. 235.

24. For an excellent analysis of pre-existing local organization in the Civil Rights Movement that parallels some of my discussion, see Aldon Morris, *The Origins of the Civil Rights Movement: Black Communities Organizing for Change* (New York: The Free Press, 1984).

25. For those interested in the evolution of SNCC, Clayborne Carson's *In Struggle, SNCC and the Black Awakening of the 1960's* (Cambridge: Harvard Univ. Press, 1981), is required reading.

26. Martin Luther King, Jr., *Where Do We Go From Here: Chaos or Community?* (Boston: Beacon Press, 1968), p. 124.

27. Ibid.

28. Ibid., p. 17.

29. Haynes Walton, *The Political Philosophy of Martin Luther King, Jr.* (Westport, Conn.: Greenwood Press, 1971), p. 93.

30. King, *Chaos or Community?*, p. 125.

31. Ibid., p. 36.

32. Walton, *Political Philosophy*, p. 92.

33. Charles Denby, *Indignant Heart: A Black Worker's Journal* (Boston: South End Press, 1978), p. 57.

34. Ibid., p. 59.

35. Ibid., p. 60.

36. Ibid., pp. 60, 62.

37. For a discussion of Bearden, see Elton Fax, *17 Black Artists* (New York: Dodd, Mead, 1971); Charles Childs, "Bearden: Identification and Identity," *Art News*, Oct. 1964, pp. 24–25, 54, 61–62; Calvin Tomkins, "Putting Something Over Something Else," *New Yorker* (no. 37, 1977), pp. 53–57; and Elsa Honig Fine, *The Afro-American Artist* (New York: Holt, Rinehart and Winston, 1973).

38. Ralph Ellison, "The Art of Romare Bearden," in R. Ellison, *Going to the Territory* (New York: Random House, 1987), pp. 236–37.

39. Cited in Childs, "Bearden: Identification and Identity," p. 62.

40. Ralph Ellison, "The World and the Jug," in Ralph Ellison,

Shadow and Act (New York: Vintage Books, 1972), p. 139 and p. 142. For an important discussion of Ellison's interpretation of folklore as living communication rather than artifact, see Robert G. O'Meally, "Riffs and Rituals: Folklore in the Work of Ralph Ellison," in *Afro-American Literature: The Reconstruction of Instruction,"* ed. Dexter Fisher and Robert B. Stepto (New York: The Modern Language Association of America, 1979), pp. 153–169.

41. Ellison, *Shadow and Act*, p. 137.

42. Cited in Childs, "Bearden," p. 61.

43. For some important overviews of black women writers, see *Home Girls: a Black Feminist Anthology*, ed. Barbara Smith (New York: Kitchen Table Women of Color Press, 1983), and *Conjuring: Black Women, Fiction and Literary Tradition*, ed. Marjorie Pryse and Hortense J. Spellers (Bloomington: Indiana Univ. Press, 1985).

44. Jerry Gonzalez, "The River Is Deep," Liner-notes for the recording, *Jerry Gonzalez and the Fort Apache Band* (Nymphenburger, W. Germany: ENJA Records, no. 4040).

45. Enriquez Fernandez, "The Children of Salsa," *Village Voice* 3 January 1984, p. 68.

46. John ("Dizzy") Gillespie pioneered fusions of Afro-North American and Afro-Cuban musical cultures. For example, listen to his 1947 "Cubana Be"/"Cubana Bop."

47. Gonzalez, "River Is Deep." For a music creator's discussion of improvisation analogous to some of my analysis of Mutuality, see Leo Smith, *notes /(8 pieces)/source/a new/ world music: creative music.* (New Haven, Conn.: Leo Smith, 1973). For example, Smith writes that, unlike highly orchestrated composed music, "the independent center of the improvisation is continuously changing depending upon the force created by individual" musicians. Improvisation is cooperative "autonomy" (p. 26). For another important discussion of these issues in music, see Marion Brown, *Recollections* (Frankfurt: Juergen A. Schmitt Publikationen, 1973).

48. C. L. R. James, *The Future in the Present* (Westport, Conn.: Lawrence Hill, 1977), p. 191.

49. Ibid., pp. 196, 201.

50. "Jackson Leads 3 Day Assault on Party's Direction," *New York Times*, 20 April 1986, p. 31. In the 1988 presidential primaries and caucuses Jackson won 29.3 percent of the vote thus tripling his share of the white vote from 1984. Apparently, the strategy of addressing issues of concern to a range of groups had borne some fruit.

Index

A. *Philip Randolph: A Biographi-*
cal Portrait (Anderson), 152 n
Abyssinian Baptist Church, 113
Africa, 126–127, 142, 160 n; Du
Bois on, 32–33, 40; Ellis in, 83;
Messenger on, 52; Schomburg
on, 96–99, 104; Washington on,
29
African culture, 126; *New Negro*
on, 70, 75; Schomburg on,
96–99
African Methodist Episcopal
Church, 113, 124
African Methodist Episcopal Zion
Church, 113
African National Congress, 147
"African Roots of the War, The"
(Du Bois), 32, 39, 115
African World, 117
Africans Abroad (Brawley), 96
Afro-American Artist, The (Fine),
161 n
Afro-American Christianity:
Nation of Islam's view of,
123–124, 127
Afro-American churches, 134
Afro-American culinary knowl-
edge: Schomburg on, 103–115
Afro-American culture, 128; G.
Jackson on, 127–128; Nation of

Islam on, 124–125; Schomburg
on, 103–115; Washington on,
29–30
Afro-American music, 140–144
Afro-American nationalism,
126–127; Cruse on, 129
Afro-Brazilian religion: and
Nation of Islam, 126
Afrocentric Idea, The (Asante),
159 n
Afro-Cuban music, 142
Agriculture: Washington on, 14,
15, 21–22, 25
Alabama: UNIA in, 118
Allison, Roger, 146
American Negro Academy, 95
Americanness, 70–74; Du Bois
on, 40
Anderson, Carlotta, 158 n
Anderson, Jervis, *A. Philip*
Randolph: A Biographical
Portrait, 152 n
Anderson, Jim, 158 n
Angelou, Maya, 140
Anti-Semitism: *Messenger* view of
Russian, 56
Aristotle: Du Bois on, 42
Arkansas: UNIA in, 118
Arts, the: *Messenger* on, 64–66,
69. *See also* culture

163

Asante, Molefi Kete, *The Afro-centric Idea*, 159 n
Asia: Du Bois on, 32; *Messenger* on, 52; Schomburg on, 97–99
Association for the Study of Negro Life and History, 119–120
Aurelius, Marcus: Du Bois on, 42
Australia: UNIA in, 117
Avrich, Paul, *The Russian Anarchists*, 150 n

Baker, Ella, 161 n
Balzac, Honoré de: Du Bois on, 42
Bambara, Toni Cade, 140
Barron, Harold, 88
Bearden, Romare, 139, 140
Black Hebrews, 112
Black Panther Party, 127, 130, 132, 136, 144, 160 n
Black Power, 131; King on, 136
Blair, Barbara, and R. Hill, *Marcus Garvey, Life and Lessons*, 159 n
Blassingame, John, 12
Blues, the, 112
Boas, Franz, 86, 158 n
Bolsheviks, 12–13; *Messenger* on, 51, 55–57
Booker T. Washington, the Making of a Black Leader, 1856–1911 (Harlan), 149 n
Boycotts: Washington's support for, 150 n
Bracey, John H., 160 n
Brawley, Benjamin, *Africans Abroad*, 96
Brazil: UNIA in, 118
Brecher, Jeremy, *Strike!*, 150 n
British Honduras: UNIA in, 117
Brown, H. Rap, 132
Brown, Marion, *Recollections*, 162 n

Brown, Sterling, *Negro Poetry and Drama and the Negro in American Fiction*, 156 n
Bruce, John: and UNIA, 120
Bruno, Giordano, 6, 149 n

Cabral, Amilcar, *Return to the Source; Selected Speeches of Amilcar Cabral*, 158 n
Calypso, 143–144
Candomblé, 126
Capitalism, 9, 115; Du Bois on, 31, 32–33, 37, 39, 41, 44–47; *Messenger* on, 52–55, 57–58; Washington on, 15–17, 22, 44–47
Carmichael, Stokely, 132
Carson, Clayborne, *SNCC and the Black Awakening of the 1960's*, 161 n
Chamberlain, Thomas, 86
Charleston, South Carolina, 105
Chenier, Clifton, 158 n
Chicago, 83, 112; Ellis on, 90–91; race riot in, 61–62; school of sociology, 154 n; UNIA in, 116
Chicago Defender, 49
Childs, Charles, 161 n
China: Du Bois on, 31–32, 34; Randolph on, 52
Civilization: Du Bois on, 31–32, 34, 36, 38–39, 41, 44–47
Colored Farmers Alliance, 13
Colson, William, 61
Communist Manifesto, The (Engels and Marx), 20
Communist Party: of South Africa, 147; of U.S.A., 138
Congress of South African Trade Unions, 147
Conjuring: Black Women, Fiction, and Literary Tradition (Pryse and Spellers), 162 n

Connecticut, 109
Correspondence: of oppressed groups, 7
Cosmopolitan environment: of Afro-Americans, 48–49
Crisis of the Negro Intellectual, The (Cruse), 129, 152 n, 154 n
Cronon, J. A., 115
Cruse, Harold, 129, 130; The Crisis of the Negro Intellectual, 129, 152 n, 154 n
Cuba, 142; UNIA in, 117, 118
Cuban music, 142
Culture, 126–127; Cruse on, 129; Du Bois on, 30–44; Ellis on, 83; Messenger on, 66–67, 68, 69; Washington on, 23–30, 46–47

Daddy Grace, 112
Dahomey: UNIA in, 117
Declaration of Independence: Du Bois on, 40
Democracy: Du Bois on, 37, 46–47; Ellis on, 89–91, 93–94; Messenger on Russian, 55–56; Schomburg on, 97; UNIA on, 118–119
Democratic Party: Messenger on, 50
Denby, Charles, 137–139; Indignant Heart: A Black Worker's Journal, 137
Detroit, 112; Schomburg on, 107
Dialect Poetry, 156 n; Ellis on, 91–92
"Did Bolshevism Stop Race Riots in Russia?" (Domingo), 56
Domingo, W. A., "Did Bolshevism Stop Race Riots in Russia?" 56; "Private Property as a Pillar of Prejudice," 53

Drake, St. Clair, 82
Du Bois, W. E. B., 10, 11, 80, 128, 130, 154 n; on Africa, 32–33, 40; "The African Roots of the War," 32, 39, 115; on Americanness, 40; on Aristotle, 42; on Asia, 32; on Aurelius, 42; on Balzac, 42; on capitalism, 31, 32–33, 37, 39, 41, 44–47; on civilization, 31–32, 34, 36, 38–39, 41, 44–47; on culture, 30–44, 46–47; on Declaration of Independence, 40; on democracy, 37, 46–47; on Dumas, 42; on education, 10, 19, 34–37; on Egyptian culture, 40; on electoral politics, 43, 46–47; Ellis praised by, 82; on Ethiopia, 40; on Garvey, 10–11, 119; on Greek culture, 40; on labor aristocracy, 32–33; uses machine analogy, 34–38, 45–46; Messenger compared with, 55; Messenger critique of, 10–11, 66–68, 69; on Plato, 35, 41; on race war, 33, 43; on racism, 31–33, 39, 43–47; on Reconstruction, 43; cites Ruskin, 38; on science, 34, 36–38; on Shakespeare, 42; on slavery, 11–12; The Souls of Black Folk, 17; cites Tagore, 36; on vanguard membership requirements, 17–20; Washington compared with, 14, 39, 44–47; on World War (First), 32–33
Du Chatellier, Marie: and UNIA, 120
Dumas, Alexander, 96; Du Bois on, 42
Dunbar, Paul Lawrence: Ellis on, 91–93

East St. Louis: race riots in, 60–61

Economic system: Du Bois on, 34–35, 37; *Messenger* on, 50–51, 52–53, 59–60, 62–64, 66–67; UNIA on, 118, 122; Washington on, 14–17, 20–24

Education: Du Bois on, 10, 19, 34–37; Ellis on, 87–89; Schomburg on, 97–102; Washington on, 24–27, 28

Egyptian culture: Du Bois on, 40

Electoral politics, 130–132; Du Bois on, 43, 46–47; Ellis on, 90–91, 94; *Messenger* on, 50–52, 66; Washington on, 15, 46–47

Elegua, 142

Ellington, Edward Kennedy "Duke," 141

Ellis, George W., 81, 82–95, 155 n; on Chicago, 90–91; on culture, 83; on democracy, 89–91, 93–94; on dialect poetry, 91–92; Du Bois on, 82; on Dunbar, 91–93; on education, 87–89; on electoral politics, 90–91, 94; on ethnology, 85–86; on evolution, 84; on French Revolution, 89, 94; on Haiti, 89, 94; *Negro Culture in West Africa*, 82, 83; on racism, 84–86; Rodgers on, 153 n; on scholarship, 84–87, 93, 94; on science, 84–87

Ellison, Ralph, 139, 140

Engels, Frederick, and K. Marx, *The Communist Manifesto*, 20

England: UNIA in, 118

Environmental issues, 147

Ethiopia, 95; Du Bois on, 40

Ethnology: Ellis on, 85–86

Evolution: Ellis on, 84; Washington on, 26

Fard, Wallace D., 123

Farm crisis, 144

Fast, Howard, 137

Father Divine, 112

Fauset, Arthur Huff, 75, 78–79, 154 n

Fauset, Jessie, 70

Fax, Elton, *17 Black Artists*, 161 n

Fernandez, Enrique, 141

Ferris, William, *Social History of the American Negro*, 96; and UNIA, 120

Fine, Elsa Honig, *Afro-American Artist, The*, 161 n

Fleming, John E., 155 n

Folk art: *New Negro* on, 78

Folk culture: and Boas, 158 n; Ellison on, 162 n; *New Negro* on, 75–79; Schomburg on, 111

Foreign policy: U.S., 146

Fort Apache Band, 141–143

Franklin, John Hope, 12, 157 n

Frazier, E. Franklin, 113

Free South Africa Activists, 145

French Revolution: Ellis on, 89, 94

Frye, Hardy, 130–132, 160 n

Garvey, Marcus, 10, 11, 81, 118, 158 n; and Du Bois, 10–11, 119; and *Messenger*, 10–11, 119. *See also* Universal Negro Improvement Association

Gates, Henry Louis, 79, 156 n

Geertz, Clifford, xi

Georgia: UNIA in, 118

Gillispie, John Birks "Dizzie," 162 n

Gramsci, Antonio, 8

Grass-roots organization, 12–13, 145

Great Chain of Being: A Study

in the History of an Idea, The
   (Lovejoy), 149 n
Greek culture: Du Bois on, 40
Greens, 147
Guatemala: UNIA in, 118

Haiti, 126; Ellis on, 89, 94;
   Nation of Islam on, 126, 160 n;
   Washington on, 25, 26
Haitian workers in Cuba: UNIA
   support for, 118
Hamilton, Charles, 132
Hamer, Fannie Lou, 9
Hansberry, Lorraine, 140
Harlan, Louis R., *Booker T.
   Washington, the Making of a
   Black Leader 1856–1911*, 149 n
Harlem, 113, 139; Garvey in,
   115; in *New Negro*, 70–73;
   Schomburg on, 109, 110; UNIA
   in, 119
Harlem Renaissance (Huggins),
   153 n
Harriet Tubman Publishing Co.,
   95
Havana: UNIA in, 116
Hayden, Robert, 70
Hearne, Lafcaido: Schomburg on,
   106
Herskovits, Melville, 70–71,
   154 n
Hill, Robert, and B. Blair, *Mar-
   cus Garvey, Life and Lessons*,
   159 n
History: Schomburg on, 99,
   100–101; UNIA on, 118
*Home Girls: A Black Feminist
   Anthology* (Smith), 162 n
Houston: race riot in, 61
Huggins, Nathan, *Harlem Renais-
   sance*, 153 n
Hurston, Zora Neale, 140

Ibsen, Henrick: *Messenger* on, 65

Illinois, 83
Improvisation, 140–141
*Indignant Heart: A Black
   Worker's Journal* (Denby), 137
Intellectuals: Cruse on, 129;
   Schomburg on, 114; in UNIA,
   119, 120–121
Ireland: and UNIA, 120
Islam, 125, 160 n. *See also* Nation
   of Islam
Italo-Ethiopian War, 95

Jackson, George, 127–129, 144;
   on Afro-American culture,
   127–128
Jackson, Jesse, 144–145, 146,
   162 n
Jamaican workers in Cuba: UNIA
   support for, 118, 119
James, C. L. R., 126, 143–144
Jews in Russia: *Messenger* on, 56
Johnson, Charles, 10, 70, 73–77,
   80, 111
Johnson, James Weldon, 72–73
Journal of Race Development, 86
Justice Department, 10

Kansas, 23
Kansas City, 112
Kenya: UNIA in, 117
King, Martin Luther, Jr., 133–
   137; on Black Power, 136; on
   Nation of Islam, 135–137

Labor aristocracy: Du Bois on,
   32–33
Ladner, Joyce, 131
Latino, Juan, 96, 156 n
Legal action: King on, 134
Lenin, Vladimir Illich, 32, 127;
   Messenger on, 51, 57
Liberia: Ellis on, 83; Randolph
   on, 52; Washington on, 25, 26

Locke, Alain, 11, 49, 69, 75, 77–78, 95; Schomburg contrasted with, 111
Logan, Rayford, 82
Lovejoy, Arthur, *The Great Chain of Being: A Study in the History of an Idea,* 149 n

Machine analogy: in Du Bois, 34–38, 45–46; in *Messenger,* 50–52, 57–58; in Washington, 26–27
Makno, Lester, 13
Malcolm X, 7
Man Furthest Down: A Record of Observation and Study in Europe, The (Washington), 150 n
Maoist models, 127
Marcus Garvey, Life and Lessons (Blair and Hill), 159 n
Martin, Tony, 115, 116
Marx, Karl, and F. Engels, *The Communist Manifesto,* 20, 29
Marxism, 16, 130, 136, 137, 144
Massachusetts, 145
Mathematics: Washington on, 26
Meier, August, *Negro Social Thought in America, 1880–1915, Racial Ideologies in the Age of Booker T. Washington,* 149 n
Messenger, 10, 11, 12, 14, 49–69, 130; on Africa, 52; on the arts, 64–66; on Asia, 52; on Bolsheviks, 55–57; on culture, 66–67, 68, 69; on democracy in Russia, 55–56; on Democratic Party, 50; Du Bois compared with, 55; Du Bois criticized by, 10–11, 66–68, 69; on economic exploitation, 59–60; on economic power, 62–64; on electoral politics, 50–52, 56;

and Garvey, 10–11, 119; on Ibsen, 65; on Jews in Russia, 56; on Lenin, 53, 57; uses machine analogy, 50–52, 57–58; on naturalism in the arts, 65–66; on race riots, 60–62; on racism, 54; on Republican Party, 50, 51; on Russia, 51, 55–58; on science, 65–67; on Trotsky, 51, 57; Washington compared with, 55, 69; on working-class unity, 54, 58–60
Mexico: UNIA in, 118, 119
Mighty Sparrow, The, 143–144
Mississippi, 113; UNIA in, 116, 118
Missouri Rural Crisis Center, 146
Montgomery Bus Boycott, 137, 138
Morris, Aldon, *The Origins of the Civil Rights Movement: Black Communities Organizing for Change,* 161 n
Muhammad, Elijah, 123–124, 125
Muhammad Speaks, 126
Mutuality, 5–9, 147–148

NAACP, see National Association for the Advancement of Colored People
Nacion, La, 117
Nation of Islam, 123–127, 128, 129, 130; on Afro-American Christianity, 123–124, 127; on Haiti, 126, 160 n; King on, 135–136, 137
National Association for the Advancement of Colored People (NAACP), 138
National Baptist Convention, U.S.A., 113, 124
National boundaries, 147–148; UNIA on, 116, 121

Naturalism in art: *Messenger* on, 65–66
Negro Actors Guild, 95
Negro Culture in West Africa (Ellis), 82, 83
Negro Poetry and Drama and the Negro in American Fiction (Brown), 156 n
Negro Society for Historical Research, 95, 156 n
Negro Thought in America, 1880–1915, Racial Ideologies in the Age of Booker T. Washington (Meier), 149 n
Negro World, 116
New Negro, The, 10, 12, 14, 49, 69–80, 111–112; on African culture, 70, 75; on folk art, 78; on folk culture, 75–79; on Harlem, 70–73; on New York, 72; on urbanization, 73–77; on Y.M.C.A., 74
New South, 17
New York, 113; *New Negro* on, 72; UNIA in, 116
Newton, Huey P., 160 n
Nicaragua: UNIA on, 120
North American Farmers Alliance, 145
notes /(8 pieces)/source/a new/ world/music: creative music (Smith), 162 n
Nuclear war, 146

O'Meally, Robert G., 162 n
Oral tradition: Schomburg on, 98
Origins of the Civil Rights Movement: Black Communities Organizing for Change, The (Morris), 161 n
Owen, Chandler, 10, 49, 68

Park, Robert, 70, 113
Philadelphia: race riots in, 60–61

Plato: Du Bois on, 35, 41; and Washington, 27
Poland, 147
Political Philosophy of Martin Luther King, Jr. (Walton), 135
Powell, Bud, 142
Pozo, Chano, 141–142
Prensa, La, 117
"Private Property as a Pillar of Prejudice" (Domingo), 53
Progressive Party, 83
Pryse, Marjorie, and H. Sellers, *Conjuring: Black Women, Fiction, and Literary Tradition*, 162 n
Puerto Rico, 95, 142
Pushkin, Aleksander, 96

Raboteau, Albert, 12
Race riots: in Chicago, 61–62; in East St. Louis, 60–61; in Houston, 61; in Russia, 56; *Messenger* on, 56, 60–62
Race war: Du Bois on, 33
Racism: Du Bois on, 31–33, 39, 43–45; Ellis on, 84–86, 90; *Messenger* on, 53–54; Washington on, 14–17, 20–21, 27–28, 43–45
Rachleff, Peter, 12
Rainbow Coalition, 144–148
Randolph, A. Philip, 10, 49, 68, 152 n; on Liberia, 52
Recollections (Brown), 162 n
Reconstruction, 13; Du Bois on, 43
Religion: UNIA on, 117
Republican Party, 83; *Messenger* on, 50, 51
Return to the Source: Selected Speeches of Amilcar Cabral (Cabral), 158 n
Rhode Island, 109
Robeson, Paul, 137

Rodgers, J. A.: on Ellis, 153 n; and UNIA, 120
Royce, Josiah: Du Bois on, 35
Rural/urban continuity: Schomburg on, 111–114
Ruskin, John: Du Bois cites, 38
Russia, 12; *Messenger* on, 51, 55–58
Russian Anarchists, The (Avrich), 150 n

San Juan, 95
Sanneh, Lamin O., *West African Christianity: The Religious Impact*, 160 n
Santo Domingo: Washington on, 25, 26
Scholarship: Ellis on, 84–87, 93, 94; Schomburg on, 101–102
Schomburg, Arturo, 81–82, 95–115, 142, 156 n, 157 n; on Africa, 96–99, 104; on African culture, 96–99; on Afro-American culinary knowledge, 103–115; on Afro-American culture, 114; on Asia, 97–99; on democracy, 97; on Detroit, 107; on education, 97–102; on folk culture, 111; on Harlem, 109, 110; on Hearne, 120; on history, 99, 100–101; on intellectuals, 114; C. Johnson contrasted with, 111; Locke contrasted with, 111; on oral tradition, 98; on rural/urban continuity, 111–114; on scholarship, 101–102; on science, 95, 98, 100; on slave narratives, 100; on slavery, 112; and UNIA, 119; on urbanization, 112; on West Indies, 104; on Wister, 106

Schomburg Center for Research in Black Culture, 95
Science: Du Bois on, 36–38; Ellis on, 84–87; *Messenger* on, 65–67; Schomburg on, 95, 98, 100
SCLC. *See* Southern Christian Leadership Conference
17 Black Artists (Fax), 161 n
Shakespeare: Du Bois on, 42
Shange, Ntoshake, 140
Slave narratives: Schomburg on, 100
"Slave Ship, The" (Turner), 38
Slavery: Du Bois on, 11–13; Washington on, 11, 28; Schomburg on, 112
Smith, Abdullahi, 160 n
Smith, Barbara, *Home Girls: A Black Feminist Anthology*, 162 n
Smith, Bessie, 111, 158 n
Smith, Leo, *notes /(8 pieces)/ source/a new/ world music: creative music*, 162 n
Smoke (Turgenev), 94
SNCC. *See* Student Non-Violent Coordinating Committee
SNCC and the Black Awakening of the 1960's (Carson), 161 n
Social History of the American Negro, A (Ferris), 96
Socialist Party of Sicily: Washington on, 150 n
Solidarity Union, 147
Souls of Black Folk, The (Du Bois), 17
South Africa, 147; UNIA in 117, 118, 119
Southern Christian Leadership Conference (SCLC), 138
Spellers, Hortense, J., and M. Pryce, *Conjuring: Black*

Women, Fiction and Literary Tradition, 162 n
Spontaniety: organizational basis of, 13
Stalinism, 144
Strike! (Brecher), 150 n
Student Non-Violent Coordinating Committee (SNCC), 9, 130–132, 138, 161 n

Tagore, Rabindrinath: Du Bois cites, 35
Technology: Washington on, 15, 21–22, 25–27, 30. *See also* machine analogy
Timbuctu, 96
Tomkins, Calvin, 161 n
Trinidad: UNIA in, 117
Trotsky, Leon: *Messenger* on, 51, 57
Turgenev, Ivan, *Smoke*, 94
Turner, Joseph, M., "The Slave Ship," 38

UNIA. *See* Universal Negro Improvement Association
United Democratic Front, 147
Universal Negro Improvement Association (UNIA), 49, 81, 115–122, 132, 137, 147, 158 n; in Africa, 117–118, 119; in Alabama, 118; in Arkansas, 118; in Australia, 117; in Brazil, 118; in British Honduras, 117; and Bruce, 120; in Chicago, 116; in Cuba, 117, 118; in Dahomey, 117; on democracy, 117; and Du Chatellier, 120; in England, 118; and Ferris, 120; in Georgia, 118; in Guatemala, 118; supports Haitian workers in Cuba, 118; in Harlem, 119; in Havana, 116; on history, 118; intellectuals in, 119, 120–121; and Ireland, 120; supports Jamaican workers in Cuba, 118, 119; in Kenya, 117; in Mississippi, 116; in Mexico, 118, 119; on national boundaries, 116, 121; in New York, 116; and Nicaragua, 120; on religion, 117; and Rodgers, 120; and Schomburg, 119; in Trinidad, 117; in Venezuela, 118; in Wales, 118; in West Africa, 118; and Woodson, 119
Up From Slavery: An Autobiography (Washington), 151 n
Urbanization: *New Negro* on, 73–77; Schomburg on, 112

Vai peoples: Ellis on, 83
Vanguard Perspective, 3–5, 13, 14, 147–148
Venezuela: UNIA in, 118
Vodun, 126

Wales: UNIA in, 118
Walker, Alice, 140
Walton, Haynes, *Political Philosophy of Martin Luther King, Jr.*, 135
Washington, Booker T., 10, 11, 14–17, 20–30, 118, 128, 130; on Africa, 29; on agriculture, 14, 15, 21–22, 25; supports boycotts, 150 n; on capitalism, 15–17, 22, 44–47; on culture, 23–30, 46–47; Du Bois compared with, 10–11, 14, 39, 44–47; on economic system, 14–17, 20–24; on electoral politics, 15, 46–47; on Haiti, 25, 26; on Liberia, 25, 26; uses machine analogy, 26–27;

Washington, Booker T., *cont.*
The Man Furthest Down: A Record of Observation and Study in Europe, 150 n; on mathematics, 26; *Messenger* compared with, 10–11, 55, 69; and Plato, 27; on racism, 14–17, 20–21, 27–28, 43–45; on Santo Domingo, 25, 26; on science, 30; on slavery, 11, 28; and socialism, 150 n; on technology, 15, 21–22, 25–27, 30; *Up From Slavery: An Autobiography*, 151 n; on vanguard leadership, 14–17
West Africa, 142; UNIA in, 118
West African Christianity: The Religious Impact (Sanneh), 160 n
West Indies: Schomburg on, 104
Winston, Michael, 82
Wirth, Louis, 113
Wister, Owen: Schomburg on, 106
Woodson, Carter, G., 156 n; and UNIA, 119
Working class unity: *Messenger* on, 54, 59–60
World War (First), Du Bois on, 32–33

Zimbabwe, 96
Zydeco music, 158 n